DATE DUE			

70560
Newman

St. Procopius College Library
Maple Ave. and College Road
Lisle, Illinois

LIBERALISM

and the Retreat from Politics

BY WILLIAM J. NEWMAN
The Futilitarian Society

LIBERALISM

and the Retreat from Politics

by

WILLIAM J. NEWMAN

WITHDRAWN

GEORGE BRAZILLER
NEW YORK

HM
24
N4

Copyright © 1964 by William J. Newman
All rights in this book are reserved.
For information address the publisher,
George Braziller, Inc.
215 Park Avenue South
New York 3, New York

FIRST PRINTING

Library of Congress Catalog Card Number: 64-10787

PRINTED IN THE UNITED STATES OF AMERICA

70560

TO

Betty and Vickie

WHO SUSTAINED THE BURDEN OF

THIS BOOK

Acknowledgments

In writing a work of this kind, many debts are contracted. For his long and arduous work on this book, I should especially like to express my thanks to Professor Sidney Black of Boston University. He took an unruly manuscript, and through a series of collaborative seminars, reformed it in the interests of clarity. There are few pages that have not benefited from his generous willingness to spend many hours of his time in this effort.

I should also like to acknowledge my debt to Professor Hubert Gibbs, Chairman of the Department of Government, Boston University, not only for reading the manuscript and making many valuable suggestions but also for providing essential financial aid. Mr. Edwin Seaver of George Braziller, Inc., also gave the manuscript close and careful attention which went well beyond the call of duty.

Two old friends have helped bring this book into being. Dr. Byron H. Waksman (whose editorial presence has, I hope, haunted these pages) and Dr. William C. Powell have both provided support for this venture, each in his own way. Without their comradeship this work would never have been written. I must also express my deep debt to Mr. George Lichtheim of London who not only made it possible for me to begin writing in this field but whose transatlantic letters have been a constant stimulus to thought—which is not to say that he will agree with the theme of this book!

Professor Lewis Coser of Brandeis University, and Professor Scott Miyakawa read parts of the manuscript in its early stages and made significant suggestions. I must thank Mrs. Helena Lothrop and Mrs. Sheila Armstrong for their rapid and efficient secretarial work.

The bulk of Chapter 6 was originally an article in *Dissent* —a journal which under the editorship of Professors Irving Howe and Lewis Coser kept the flag of radicalism flying when radicalism was out of fashion—and is reprinted here with their kind permission.

To my parents, I owe, of course, a very special debt, for they made this book possible by their constant support of my enterprises over a long period of time.

To my wife and child, Betty and Vickie, I owe something which far transcends the obligations most writers have to their family. As the creators of the most important society of all, they are the real authors of this work.

I alone am responsible, of course, for any errors of fact or opinion.

W. J. N.

Contents

Introduction

Liberalism has passed through many phases since the turn of the century. Although some of these show it at war with itself or contradicting its own past, liberalism has nevertheless consistently possessed a sense of relevance to its times and an active spirit closely tied to concrete historical reality. In its most recent phase, however, beginning in the late 1940's and continuing up to the present, this sense, this spirit would seem to have become so diminished that one may even wonder if liberalism is not something carried over from a "dead" past.

What is its relevance to our present historical situation? This question is more difficult to answer now than at any time in the long history of liberal and radical[1] thought in America. The difficulty arises in part from our disillusion with its past, in part from the very success of liberalism. Just because it has become such a widespread doctrine, it has lost much of its specific ideological meaning and become a set of vague assumptions by which many live but which are too general to involve us in paying the costs of action. It has thus become the chief victim of what has been speciously called "the end of ideology." Yet, if liberalism is dead, then freedom is threatened in its very existence, because liberalism is the

[1] The terms liberal and radical are here used in tandem not because there are no significant differences between them but because today the differences are less considerable than the similarities. David Riesman as a liberal, and the late C. Wright Mills as a radical, for example, despite their important disagreements, have in common fundamental ways of thinking and criticizing American society. One of the chief qualities of contemporary liberalism and radicalism is this tendency to coalesce on the key problems of American society. Therefore, in the following pages, as a convenience we shall use the terms *liberal* and *liberalism* to indicate this common ground.

concept of Western thought uniquely concerned with the idea of freedom and change.[2]

Those who point to the irrelevance of liberalism today because it is a doctrine of the past fail to realize that, more than any other set of social and political ideas, it is capable of shedding its skin, of finding a new form, precisely because it values freedom so highly. Of course, there are always those who stand around fascinated by the dead skin and murmur, "The poor thing has died." But the poor thing hasn't died, although it does have problems. Today in America there are indications of a new form of liberalism, a new search for freedom. It is our purpose in this book to consider some of the problems and dilemmas this new search presents.

Its main representative is the school of social critics that has grown up in America since the end of the war. Although the profession of social critic and the ideology of liberalism do not necessarily coincide—and it must be emphasized that to be a social critic is not enough to make one a liberal, or any other kind of political animal, for that matter—those who have made significant contributions have been liberals of one shape or another. Liberal values have informed their intellectual endeavors throughout; indeed, they have undertaken their work in order to find some basis in our present society for the values and concepts of liberalism. Their desire to find a new

[2] A problem of terminology can often arise when the word "liberal" is used, particularly among those who look at America from the perspective of European political thought. The liberalism which is being discussed here is the way of thinking that arose in American life toward the end of the nineteenth century as a reform movement and ideology and that aimed to achieve greater freedom and equality mainly but not exclusively through government intervention of one kind or another. The variety and phases of this movement are notorious; the differences of approach—and the confusions of thought—have been many. (See Eric Goldman's *Rendezvous with Destiny* [New York: Alfred A. Knopf, Inc., 1952].) The liberal movement and ideology we are discussing is essentially a twentieth-century phenomenon which is fundamentally at variance with nineteenth-century liberalism and in fact arose in direct contradiction to it.

and stable basis for the belief in freedom above all other values supports the claim that they have not only established a school of social criticism but created something more important—a new search for freedom.

Americans in general and liberals in particular owe much to these critics; in a time of fear, distrust, and doubt they have attempted to keep the idea of freedom alive and to find ways of making it operative in the new conditions of our time. David Riesman and C. Wright Mills especially have each in his own way acted as significant and responsible leaders. Altogether, the social critics have been a most potent influence in the last decade; particularly among the intellectuals and middle class they have refashioned the image of America, and in doing so have created a whole new way for us to conceive of freedom and its possibilities in the world in which we live.

Our middle class has gone to school with these critics, who have attempted to deal not merely with particular areas of American life but with the whole of it, with everything from the family to politics. Their effort to create holistic theories has given importance to their ideas. They have sought truths men can live by and have sought to teach us how to think about and what to expect from politics, our personalities, and society. They have tried to think through the whole problem of freedom in its most fundamental and sweeping aspects.

But for all their achievements in a difficult time, they may be said to have led liberal thought into some wrong and even dangerous paths. It is these paths we shall study in the following pages.

One must have a certain sympathy and appreciation for the attempts of the social critics to delineate the problems and the nature of freedom in our time. Their descriptions are not altogether inaccurate, and their pessimism is certainly not unwarranted. If they are correct, it is all the more important to understand the implications of their conceptions—implications of which these critics themselves are not always aware. The freedom they offer may be the only one possible today, but if so, it is a most impoverished and fragile one.

But are there indeed no alternatives? Is it not possible to conceive of freedom in less apocalyptic terms than those frequently employed by the social critics? Are there not limited, concrete, and yet significant gains to be made in the arena of politics that can make freedom once again a matter of public life rather than an assertion against one's fellowmen? (Fellowmen? They are better described by that ominous existentialist term "The Other.") Can liberalism enter into a struggle with the disarray of our public life and create new forms for freedom? To consider these questions is to raise the issue of politics in all its various forms. It is to ask whether freedom would not become more meaningful if it were conceived in terms of the events of public life.

But to raise such a question is also to ask if our political life is capable of providing the means by which specific action can be taken on a level beyond that of a purely technical game of Ins and Outs. If it is not possible for the liberal to enter meaningfully once again into public life, or for public events to lend significance to his belief in freedom, and if it is not possible for him to recognize his fellowman rather than The Other in public life, then his own life will be poor and barren.

It is the assumption of this work that the relationship of the liberal to public life is crucial. The analysis in the following chapters will turn on that problem. The first group of chapters will show how the ideas of the social critics on freedom relate to questions of history and society; those following will consider the implications of their ideas for politics. Such a discussion can hardly be complete or definitive. But if it does nothing more than demonstrate a need for the return of the liberal to public life and politics, it will have achieved its purpose.

America is now entering into a new era characterized by problems radically different from those of the past fifteen years. The postwar period has now come to an end. The position and policies that America successfully established in those years are no longer the significant issues. This shift into a new historical epoch presents both responsibilities and opportunities for the liberal. In a context freighted with opportunities for change he must create a fresh policy, a fresh ideology to expand freedom and make it meaningful in our particular society.

To understand the dimensions of that task it is necessary to reject the restrictive concept of freedom that contemporary social critics have created. Hopefully, then, the liberal will be in a position both to absorb the insights of the social critics and turn away from their myopic and static concerns. He will create a more expansive concept of freedom, not because it promises either a world remade or a special and secure world for the individual, but because it is a part of the events and situations of history, society, and politics.

LIBERALISM

and the Retreat from Politics

1

The Loss of History

Historical meaning is often confused with the cult of tradition or the taste
for the past. In fact, for the individual as for collectivities, the future is the
primary category. . . . The time we are living is defined for us by the trends
we discern in it. Formerly, perhaps, for peoples without any historical consciousness, it was a closed totality, today it is the moment of an evolution, the
means of a conquest, the origin of a will. To live historically is to locate
oneself with reference to a double transcendency.

RAYMOND ARON*

Freedom is always in question because it is the nature of
freedom to question itself. But it becomes more doubtful, and
more implausible as a concrete idea, when history ceases to be
its ally. Historical writing is not a pastime, not a matter of
antiquarianism, but a means of thinking about the possibilities of achieving political and social ends. It not only tells us
where we have been or where we are, but where we will be. It
holds out a promise of things to come, good and bad. For
modern man at least it is virtually impossible to imagine a
society without history. But at the same time we may lose our
history, lose our sense of meaningful relationship to a significant past and our hope of a future that embodies our desires.

Can the idea of freedom survive the loss of history? Can
freedom continue to exist as a concrete social reality, rather
than an airy abstraction, when the present is not conceived in

* Raymond Aron, *Introduction to the Philosophy of History* (Boston: Bea-
con Press, 1961).

terms of a historical continuum or when a new era that may
be beginning promises victory to the enemies of freedom?

The answers to such questions lie deep in the cultural and
intellectual history of Western societies. That there has been
a loss of history in some sense seems clear; as Stephen Grau-
bard, editor of *Daedalus,* has put it:

Never before have so many men worked to collect documents,
edit correspondence, and describe what others thought and did.
For all the century's historical consciousness, however, it lacks the
simple faith of a Thucydides who believed that the future, if it
did not duplicate the past, would at least resemble it, and that
this was the reason for writing history. . . . The twentieth-century
historian . . . is disinclined to believe that any of [his research] is
in any way relevant to today's problems. He tends to pursue history in and for itself. . . . There is no idea more congenial to
the twentieth century than one which suggests that it is an epoch
unique in world history. . . . This is the badge of its inordinate
pride; also, perhaps, the symbol of its ignorance.[1]

The overt recognition of the loss of history is one of the
key elements of liberal thought since World War II and occurred in sharp reaction to the totalitarian's use (and abuse)
of history to serve the ends of his movement. As Hannah
Arendt has pointed out, it was the mark of totalitarianism to
look on history as a secret key and to see it as the eternal lad-
der for movement qua movement.[2] The experience we have
had with totalitarianism has made us wary of history as a key
to anything. It can even be viewed as a developmental system
of iron laws that rob men of liberty. But to reject the repug-
nant story of our past is to reject history as a way of seeing and
hypostatizing man. A study of the ways we have lost history
will reveal the loss to be one of the characteristic qualities of

[1] *Daedalus,* Fall, 1961, pp. 621-622.
[2] See Hannah Arendt, *The Origins of Totalitarianism* (New York: Meridian
Books, 1951).

the present as well as one of the crucial problems facing those who are concerned with the subject of freedom.

The problem of the relationship of history to freedom and the processes of change is, of course, an old one;[3] sociologists and anthropologists as well as economists and the historians themselves have grappled with it in general terms since the nineteenth century. At issue here, however, is not the academic but the liberal mind; and to understand its efforts it will be necessary first to look at the way history and freedom were once tied together, second the way we lost history, and finally the way this loss is expressed in liberal thought today. We will then understand the tremendous handicap, the lack of past and future, that the new search for freedom must bear.

The Relationship of History to the Idea of Freedom

The modern idea of freedom and history came into being in the late seventeenth century and developed in the eighteenth and nineteenth centuries. Thus the relationship between the two has always been close. At the beginning the relationship between the two was, to be sure, ambiguous. But as the belief in history became more positive and better conceived, the idea of freedom came under its influence. Eventually the two could hardly be separated.[4]

[3] It is a problem that also includes a significant debate on historicism. There is no need here to engage in that debate, for certainly the dangers of historicism have been made clear. Here it is only necessary to say: (a) The use of history need not bind men so that they are robbed of their freedom but on the contrary it can be used to increase it. (b) The exact way in which history should be studied with this in mind is an important problem which has not been considered as it deserves by the modern liberal. The purpose of this chapter is to show why he has not done so, and the significance of his not having done so, rather than to engage in a discussion on historicism. It is time now to move beyond that debate.

[4] It is not, of course, claimed that the conservatives have not sought the sanction of history for their ideas of fixity. But, leaving aside the problem that the fact of historical change creates for a conservative historian, it is clear

Begin with Locke, one of the originators of the modern idea of freedom. Writing at the end of the seventeenth century, he conceived of freedom as a state of being that was a fact of nature rather than of history and that was the essence of man no matter what his historical condition. Man in a state of nature, man independent of history, created constitutional safeguards, without the assistance of historical change. For Locke a political constitution was a response to a rational calculation of interest rather than the result of historical development. Yet he did not dispense with history, even if we can no longer recognize it as such. Although in his ahistorical mind the state of nature may well have been a metaphor with no significant existence in reality, the very fact that he could only conceive of the creation of a free society as an act existing sometime in the past indicates that to him freedom had its history, that changes in its structure could only take place in a historical framework. The free society was not a natural event, but a man-made event, and as such a part of man's history.[5]

But certainly Locke's concept is not history as we now interpret it, and the gulf between his view and those which followed is a significant indication of the changes that have occurred in modern times and that have shown that freedom and history are one. Locke could and did assume a static uni-

that even though the study of history may be useful to those of any ideological persuasion, it is a necessary study for those who are concerned with the nature and problems of freedom. This affinity is indicated by E. H. Carr's comments: "History properly so-called can be written only by those who find and accept a sense of direction in history itself. . . . A society which has lost belief in its capacity to progress in the future will quickly cease to concern itself with its progress in the past." E. H. Carr, *What Is History?* (New York: Alfred A. Knopf, Inc., 1962). Such a relationship of history to freedom does not, equally, reflect on the primary responsibility of the historian to his task of accurate and scrupulous discovery of the facts.

[5] For these two aspects of Locke's thought and for his concepts of history, see R. G. Collingwood, *The Idea of History* (New York: Oxford University Press, Inc., 1956).

verse; he anticipated the eighteenth-century belief that history had reached or was about to reach its fruition.[6] But the eighteenth century itself was to provide the very dynamics that brought the modern conception of history into being. When Locke assumed a static society, it was already undergoing the transition into the industrial revolution, which proved one thing at least, namely that history had decidedly not reached its fruition and that change was the permanent lot of man. Locke was not the last political thinker to ignore the events happening under his nose, but the result of his ignorance was that never again was it possible to think of freedom as Locke thought of it—as an essence of man—or of a free society as he thought of it, once and for all an act of man. The industrial revolution proved that man could lose his liberty—that Britons could be slaves—and that a free society could only be founded on the basis of historical forces.

From the industrial revolution on, man himself was seen as a product of past forces. Freedom was no longer the result of a social contract but of dynamic change which man may or may not direct. If man directed the historical process, then he must attend to it. He must use his rationality in the cause of freedom. If he did not, then he must await with more or less passivity for the freedom that those forces might create. In either case, the result was the same in at least one respect. The assurance of freedom had to be sought in the turn of events. No longer could it be postulated in an abstract, nonexistent state of nature; rather, it had to be proven by the facts of history. If man is free, it is because he struggled out of slavery in the past, or because he would struggle out of slavery in the future. The proof that man is free was no longer to be found

---

[6] One must beware, of course, of making easy historical judgments. Henry Vyverberg's *Historical Pessimism in the French Enlightenment* (Cambridge, Mass.: Harvard University Press, 1958) indicates that optimism was far from the only current of thought in the eighteenth century.

in what man is—his essence—but in what he had been or was to be.

The consequences of such a shift were many and sweeping. To look to the process of history is to discover the nature of freedom. It is not enough to say that man shall be free; history must cooperate. Hence, freedom became less independent of its environment and more intermixed with the nature of society as a whole; freedom and society became two sides of the same coin. Equally important, the form of society determined in part the specific and concrete nature of freedom, rather than the other way around, as Locke had postulated with his social contract. Further, if a man ceased to be independent of society but could only be free in society, then it was obligatory for him to consider the whole society of which he was a part if he wished to change the situation. Constitutionalism ceased to be a sufficient safeguard; it became necessary to be part of a group to express one's freedom, to be a trade unionist, to be a businessman. Thoreauvianism was no longer sufficient.

Relativity came into society with history and affected the idea of freedom, as it did everything else. What was freedom? It varied in different places and under different circumstances. True, a core definition might be possible, but such a definition would mean nothing outside the context to which it was applied. Freedom now had as many meanings as there were societies; as many meanings as there were historical epochs— thus, the need to redefine, rethink, and reestablish its content for every age. The struggles for constitutional freedom and for majority rule by universal suffrage that took place at the beginning of the nineteenth century took another form in the twentieth century when the problem became economic rather than political.

This shift to a historical approach created the need for the thematic construction of historical systems; the nineteenth century, therefore, became a century of system-makers like Buckle, Spencer, and Marx. With good reason too, for without such a system at one's elbow one was figuratively no place. Without a system that extrapolated the past and present into the future, there was no future. For those concerned with freedom it was necessary to invent a solid system to demonstrate that the forces for freedom in society would continue to work. Historical systems were a necessity, the basis for a belief in freedom.[7]

The awareness of history posed the question: If man is not born free in a state of nature, how is it possible to believe in his freedom? The answer now given lay in the assumption that growth or the possibility of growth within a historical context and as a result of historical change made freedom possible.

But what if belief in history is lost? The nineteenth-century mind would not and did not find it possible to contemplate such a possibility. Today we put history to the question. As a consequence we ask what the phrase "the loss of history" can mean.

Ways of Losing History

In one sense history cannot be lost, since facts and forces persevere. They do not cease just because of our beliefs and attitudes toward them. But even though history continues to be the dustbin of time, the idea of history may cease to have meaning for us.

The loss of history in this sense can take three forms. First, history may be regarded as a condition of men and societies

[7] Naturally, historical systems could be used and were used for other purposes than to prove that freedom had a future. In an age dominated by the discovery of the historical method, the use of history to think about any aspect of society and social change was a necessity.

whose past is seen as largely irrelevant to their present reality, and whose past problems and solutions have little relation to the problems and possible solutions of the present. As a result, the past takes on more and more the quality of antiquarianism, the type fostered by slick historical periodicals aimed at a nostalgic middle-class audience. The past is in frames, its force spent, an era ended. Although its influence may linger, it does so in the way in which a monument stands—immobile. Thus the immediate past possesses a closed quality with its own unique characteristics giving it a "place" in history. Consequently, it is of necessity and by definition divorced from the present.

The present is then seen as a situation in which almost completely new forces are at work. They are self-propelling, autonomous. They may draw their original sustenance from the past, but they seem to have now become distinctive, unique, cutting the present off from the period immediately preceding it. As new forces, they present new problems, impossible to evaluate in terms of past forces; meaning is derived, if at all, from the situation itself. Generalizations about the trends of a culture, a society, will no longer do. They cannot help us to arrive at an understanding about the meaning of these new forces. Therefore extrapolation from the present without benefit of history takes precedence over extrapolation from the past.

All societies, at all times and to some degree, go through such a process of shedding history. The normal process of change and development are the very characteristics of history. There are always new forces at work and the past is always in the process of becoming irrelevant. But the process of shedding history is one thing, the loss of history is another. In the one case, history is still conceived of as a set of trends of which a society is a part; that is why history "makes sense," why it can explain our situation. In the other, the discontinuity between past and present becomes hard and fast, and when such a discontinuity occurs in the "present," then one can talk about a loss of history.[8] Absurdity becomes the condition of man.

The loss of history takes a second form when the future ceases to be anything different from the present. It lacks the dimension of expectation to mark it off from the present. Thus the present becomes the only place in which men can live. History can, of course, be the story of repetition too, but when it is seen as repetition to the extent that no significantly new phenomena are likely to appear, and when it seems likely that present problems will continue fundamentally unresolved, then it is possible to say that the essence of history—change—is lost. In this situation a society may even be seen as developing the logic of its own internal dynamics, confining itself to the limits of the curve of its own known trajectory. For nothing new, unique, no important innovation, can occur; society lives constantly in its own present. Events may happen, but they do not deflect society; they become the subject matter of a chronicle, not a history. The dynamics of Dewey yields to the stasis of Zen. Society becomes then a gigantic gyroscope; impervious to new ways of doing things, in a very real sense it is standing still even as it revolves.

Such a possibility forbids contemplation; there is a certain horror in it. Men are more enterprising than they sometimes

[8] Whether the difference is one of degree or quality is hardly worth discussing. A more important question is whether the West has ever experienced such a period of loss before our own time. If such a question can scarcely be considered here, it can still be said that ever since the idea of history developed in the eighteenth century the sense of discontinuity has never been sharp enough to make the past irrelevant; hence the great growth of history as a study in the nineteenth century. But it must also be said that the disorder and crisis of the industrial revolution in early nineteenth-century England almost had such an effect; the intellectual results are well-known.

seem to be even to themselves. But it is nevertheless true that
the future-as-change can become so opaque that men cannot
see, cannot imagine that there will be any important changes,
cannot believe that the future will be interestingly, importantly different. Such beliefs are probably wrong; history just
does not operate that way. It is the record of surprises. Something new and important is bound to happen. But even if that
is granted, no answer to the problem of the future will have
been given. For to convince men that the future will be different, that they live in history, it is necessary to tell them how
the future will be different, to give them a concrete idea of
what changes the future will bring.

When it is no longer possible to imagine logical alternatives, alternatives that are feasible and for which historical
reasons can be given, this second form of the loss of history
occurs. It is at such a time that utopias become popular.
Utopias are always possible and should be, insofar as they
reflect real developments of new social forms, new social structures. But when the future becomes a dead end, utopian
thinking in its pejorative sense becomes the only way of getting out of the present and becomes itself a symptom of the
loss of history. Thus the future becomes fixed and the future
as the history-of-change comes to an end.

The third form of the loss of history occurs when the future
is seen as promising the victory to those forces threatening the
values an individual or a society considers to be fundamental
to a satisfying existence. The loss in this case consists in understanding only too well the vastness and impersonality of approaching change. Therefore, the individual turns away from
the future as well as from the past which is responsible for
that future. Withdrawn, detached, with a sort of gloomy interest, he observes the unfolding of history. Since the possibility of realizing his objectives is statistically slight, his interest

dims to the level of the academic at best, and at worst darkens to an "I-told-you-so." Optimism—at least, seeing opportunities for choice in the future—is absent. But if optimism about the future is not possible, then thought about the future becomes a process of shrugging one's shoulders. Pessimism about the future is the surest way of putting oneself outside of history.

The loss of history is not, therefore, amnesia; never have the archives bulged as they do today. Instead it is an attitude characteristic of an entire society or at least of its thinking members.[9]

The Problem of Freedom

The loss of history threatens the liberal with a loss of freedom because the constant possibilities for experiment offered by history cease to exist for him. Discreet, constructive change is essential to freedom. Without the ability to choose, the liberal is locked in stasis. To break out he must find some reason to believe that history offers him some hope of development, that it still exists as development.

Rather than try to redefine an old tradition, the liberal must use the past to see freedom in the context of its present historical epoch and in the context of change occurring within that epoch. If he can do so he will be able to show that choice is possible today, that it will affect the future, and that it will make the future an open one. The liberal today inevitably wonders if the idea of freedom has any meaning, if it

[9] In this situation the historian finds it more difficult than usual to perform his customary public role (as distinct from his strictly professional role) of presenting the past, or rewriting the past, to tell the present what the line of historical change is most likely to be. Instead he tends either to become more strictly professional or to laud or disparage the past as an essence rather than an existence, as finished and done so that it can be retailed complete and finished, tied up in a pretty package, and sold with the knowledge that no one will be disturbed by any mention of the strife that accompanies the creation of something new.

has not become one of those pieces of baggage from a dead past, functionless and irrelevant. But if he can establish some trends from the past at work in the society of today that will affect the future, and make it a place of change rather than a place where change is foreclosed, then he can work within public life and pursue the idea of freedom whether or not it is recognized and actively sought in his society. The liberal, therefore, must try to find a future which will be a place of experiment and change, of history as the story of development.

In one sense the liberal cannot lose history no matter how hard he tries; for it is impossible to think of freedom as static, as Locke once thought of it before the rise of historical thinking. On the other hand, the depth and rate of historical change can vary. Even a partial loss of history in any of its three forms (the break with the past, the future as repetition, and the future as destructive of freedom) can reduce freedom to its minimum content. Certainly it is possible to be gratified that we have today in America and in the West in general large areas of liberty that other peoples are denied. Perhaps we can in fact live with a freedom that has no history. The age of historical systems may be over. But let us at least be aware that if we do attempt to live without history, then we are limiting freedom.

The End of Historical Patterns

What is the situation of liberal thought today? Does it possess a view of history as a meaningful continuum offering the promise of development or does it simply offer a blank where history should be?

Among American intellectuals two lines of thinking reflect the discontinuity between past, present, and future: The first of these is seen in those writings in which the idea of modern history as a concept comes to an end; the second, in those that offer little or no hope for the future of freedom from the conclusions they draw about American society today. The first group, represented by Heilbroner and Arendt, tend to put their emphasis on the end of a historical pattern. The second group, represented by the social critics like Riesman and Mills, tend to put their emphasis on those features of American society responsible for the end of dynamic development and a future overwhelmingly hostile to freedom.

Robert Heilbroner's *The Future as History* is an eloquent representative of the first line of thought. His work is perceptive precisely because it embodies a general sense of historical loss, which in this century has been a slow dissolution of certainties and the record of failures to replace them. In itself the title reveals that the future as history is now open to question.

According to Heilbroner, the sense of history itself has been demolished; there is today a lack of understanding of "the grand dynamic of history's forces in preparing the way for eventual progress." The old myths of progress and of change have disappeared and with them "a sense of positive identification with the forces that are preparing the environment of the future." Heilbroner puts the case in a sentence when he says: "Less and less are we able to locate our lives meaningfully in the pageant of history."[10] In the absence of history as a linear statement of comprehended change, only "disorientation" and "disengagement" remain; one comes to "lose one's sense of participation in mankind's journey . . . to see only a huge milling-around, a collective living-out of lives with no larger purpose than the days which each accumulates." He asserts that "unlike our forefathers who lived very much in

[10] Robert L. Heilbroner, *The Future as History* (New York: Harper & Row, 1959).

history, we ourselves appear to be adrift in an historic void."

Heilbroner's vision of history (or rather lack of history) is based on clear evidence of the played-out quality of the standard interpretations and the manifest lack of other interpretations to replace them. History goes on whether or not we have an intellectual comprehension of it: "We cannot help living in history. We can only fail to be aware of it." Yet, without intellectual distinctions between one event and another, between one change and another, history is not only meaningless but impossible.

The consequence of such a point of view forms part of the ostinato of today's liberalism: pessimism. That Heilbroner is pessimistic about freedom is a logical consequence of his denial of the future as history. The contemplation of this future creates two problems for Heilbroner as for other liberals. The first is that we will get through its events on nerve but with almost no sense of what they mean either historically or developmentally for society as a whole. Second, the little sense of historical development we still possess today reveals that the events to come are most unlikely to provide a hospitable environment for freedom, and are almost certainly opposed to the future use of even those liberties we have.

The first consideration means that freedom as a public phenomenon will cease. There will be no sense of living in a history as a process of creating and developing freedom. With no interpretation of history, no historical continuum, there will be general pessimism, a return to private affairs with the object of protecting whatever personal liberty may be left. The second consideration means simply that those social and economic forces that will form the future are in the main opposed to anything we today recognize as freedom.

The difference between society today and earlier societies, Heilbroner explains, lies in their opposing views of what history is about. The eighteenth and nineteenth centuries saw it made by social forces both predictable and benign. Private acts, even the acts of nineteenth-century individualism, took on public meaning. Today, however, our acts, public or private, are no longer identified with historical forces; we retreat to an individualism sealed off from the larger events around us in private islands of concern, a deprivation, he points out, that does not mean the loss of personal optimism, but does mean the loss of historical optimism, one that sees change for the better in the estate of man as distinct from the estate of a man, and that cannot exist apart from a faith in "the ongoing momentum of historic forces."

Heilbroner has only the slightest hope that the West will be able to move in the direction of a betterment of our whole society. The West, as he puts it, is no longer the thrust behind the spearhead of history but its target. Other people possess a sense that their societies have a future of change in front of them; we do not. The best he can offer as a philosophy suited to our society is a wry hope not of leading the forces of history under the banner of progress but simply of trying to keep the very idea of progress alive. A desperate hope at best. To achieve that aim requires the concept of history, the "point of view which [sees] the future as part of the sweep of history," and this we manifestly lack.

The future poses another kind of threat to Heilbroner. If the liberal cannot predict the future as a process of evolution, he can predict it only too well as a set of problems that threaten freedom and that come not so much from totalitarianism outside America as from the incapacity of our own society to confront the situations at home that threaten freedom today, its incapacity to alter its basic forms of behavior. He sees our society as carrying a direct and immediate threat to the individual, that of submerging him in a meaningless, uncontrolled, and uncontrollable environment that results from the technological explosion. Some effective forms of social control are necessary. It is manifest to Heilbroner (and other liberals, for that matter) that our present and customary methods of social control have failed. It is therefore necessary to respond with new methods of social control that will realize whatever degree of freedom is possible. The actual situation shows no historical trends which can give any hope for such an evolution. Quite the contrary, for while technological and economic change still occurs, methods of social control over these forces in America show no signs of change. No historical reasons exist for believing that our business-centered civilization will change its basic orientation. Heilbroner puts it neatly: "The most likely outlook is that things will go on much as they are," and that there will be an increasing "impotence and incompetence" of the individual face to face with the new facts of technology and economics.

His liberalism, although not paraded in the form of an ideology, cuts deep. All the facts point to a situation in which the individual is increasingly confused and bewildered in an environment he can neither control nor understand. Heilbroner sees the need for social control to save freedom from the threat of private and public bureaucracies that will control and subordinate the individual. Radical change in values and power are required if such a crisis is to be avoided. Yet, seeing the need for radical change and seeing historical grounds for belief in its possibility are two different things. To be radical without the help of history and its forces is to be not unlike the old-time movie in which the hero-clown walks off a cliff and keeps on walking in mid-air, unaware of his lack of contact with reality. The difference is, of course, that the radical is aware. Unfortunately he, like the hero-clown, has no alternative but to keep walking. The analogy can be carried even further. History is a road that takes one somewhere; when one suddenly walks off it, one is not only going nowhere, one *is* nowhere.

The importance of Heilbroner lies not only in his view of the consequences of such a situation but in his awareness—more articulate and historically oriented than that of other social critics—that our condition and our problems result less from institutions, economics, and technology than from our inability to think historically. Whatever the causes of that inability may be, and they are many and complex, the central focus must necessarily be on the failure to hypostatize institutions, economics, and technology as part of a changing trend of events. We know—to take a concrete example from Heilbroner—that business as a center of independent power will become more powerful as it becomes less dependent on anything but its own self-manipulated markets. But it is difficult to think of what to do about such a situation if a new scheme of control cannot be fitted into a historical framework, if it is impossible to draw on the aid of historical forces that are conceived as bringing the new scheme of control into operation. And it is more than difficult, it is impossible to be optimistic about the consequences of such a problem if there is no longer any history, any idea that change, possibilities, alternatives are in process. Then the cynics' adage, *plus ça change, plus c'est la même chose,* will indeed be true.

Heilbroner makes explicit what underlies the social criticism of the liberal today, the idea that we can know the future in terms of its institutional, economic, and technological aspects, in terms of what might be called its realia, but that we cannot know what to do about it because we have no concept of that social change or those social forces that would create the new environment necessary to order those facts. The sense of impotence derived from this historical blindness is

one of the crucial facts of political thought today among the
liberals.

The Break with the Past

Another formulation of the loss of history is more concerned with the end of the past than the end of the future,
and is even more drastic than that presented by Heilbroner.
Hannah Arendt sees a break in the history of our political
thought, having had its "definite beginnings in the teachings
of Plato and Aristotle," and having come to a "definite end"
with the theories of Marx.[11] Her scheme of things emphasizes
the gap between the realities of today and the Western tradition of political concepts, which have up to now acted as a
guide to reality. Having lost faith in the usefulness of that
tradition and in its relevance for our problems, there is no
standard or bench mark from which to begin political specu-
lation. We can no longer think about politics by moving from
traditional concepts to new concepts that are yet continuous
with the old. Not merely does Arendt insist that we have a
feeling of confusion about the present and hence the future,
but that this feeling is based on one of the prime facts of our
time, that there is no set of ideas with which and from which
we can start to think about modern politics. For example, the
founders of the American Constitution once could formulate
their ideas and needs and inventions in a traditional yet
dynamic framework giving them the certainty of some known
ideas from which to work. Today we cannot appeal to this
particular tradition in our search for new political ideas; it is
even hard to feel that the tradition of ideas established by the
Founding Fathers is of much relevance to the problems of a

[11] Hannah Arendt, *Between Past and Future* (New York: The Viking Press,
Inc., 1961).

mass society. Indeed, those ideas may—perish the thought— be a positive detriment to solving the problems of a mass society.

Arendt fixes the responsibility for the break in our tradition on totalitarianism.

... Neither the twentieth-century aftermath nor the nineteenth-century rebellion against tradition actually caused the break in our history. This sprang from a chaos of mass-perplexities on the political scene and of mass-opinions in the spiritual sphere which the totalitarian movements, through terror and ideology, crystallized into a new form of government and domination. Totalitarian domination as an established fact, which in its unprecedentedness cannot be comprehended through the usual categories of political thought, and whose "crimes" cannot be judged by traditional moral standards or punished within the legal framework of our civilization, has broken the continuity of Occidental history. The break in our tradition is now an accomplished fact. It is neither the result of anyone's deliberate choice nor subject to further decision.[12]

She suggests that our need is to invent the new without any help from an inheritance. We have no inheritance. We must conceive afresh what democracy can mean rather than extend and develop old ideas about democracy. We must know that democracy begins with the paradox of existence within a mass society. This is the problem of a technologically fertile age. Discussion from this premise marks the end of tradition in political thought. The absence of a tradition, however, leaves the liberal incapable of thinking about the politics of social change. He can only find the difficulties of society accumulating (exactly the fear expressed by Heilbroner) while society fails to develop. He simply cannot conceive what a democracy will be like under these totally new conditions, for no new themes, no new constructs will have emerged through which

[12] *Ibid.*, p. 26.

a comparison with traditional themes and constructs would give meaning. Arendt leaves the liberal contemplating a society that is forever emerging and submerging, progressively active and distractive. To be able to think about the way democracy can work in a mass society is a necessary task for the liberal today. But the past gives him no aid and can give him no aid because of our unique situation.

But totalitarianism is only one aspect of our break in tradition. It is necessary to follow Arendt one step further to another, ultimate source of our condition. As we have seen, history, if it is to have any function for men, must be seen as a process. As a process it will be seen as a system in which logic or law is at work so that arbitrary conjunctions of events do not take place. The usefulness of such a system is undeniable, since it can be used, so to speak, as a problem-solving device. In particular, the Darwinian-Marxist school of historical thought saw the process of history in such terms. They guaranteed a future—a bourgeois idea if there ever was one—by relying on the historical process. The point that is crucial for today is that the very basis of system-making was a set of assumptions that can no longer be taken as valid. Who today can believe that "history" has a sense of a particular direction —or any direction, for that matter—in some mysterious manner? We have given up belief in both straight, rising lines of development and in circular development. We are all, to paraphrase, existentialists now, for we have discovered that the only history there is is that which we choose to make, and that we can make any history we choose, that "it" gives us no guidance. We have, in a very important sense, recovered our freedom from the system-mongers, but we have also lost the possibility of believing that freedom has a steadily improving future before it. Today we have very little if any idea what its future is or whether it will have a future because we cannot postulate a process in which it is embedded.

For Arendt this dissolution of historical certainties is part of a larger dissolution of the whole concept of process.

Today the Kantian and Hegelian way of becoming reconciled to reality through understanding the innermost meaning of the entire historical process seems to be quite as much refuted by our experience as the simultaneous attempt of pragmatism and utilitarianism to "make history" and impose upon reality the preconceived meaning and law of man. . . . What is really undermining the whole modern notion that meaning is contained in the process as a whole, from which the particular occurrence derives its intelligibility, is that . . . we can take almost any hypothesis and act upon it, with a sequence or results in reality which not only make sense but *work*. This means quite literally that everything is possible not only in the realm of ideas but in the field of reality itself.[13]

She concludes, therefore, that "Kierkegaard, Marx, and Nietzsche are for us like guideposts to a past which has lost its authority." Like Heilbroner, she despairs of the society we have: "In the situation of radical world-alienation, neither history nor nature is at all conceivable. This twofold loss of the world . . . has left behind it a society of men who, without a common world which would at once relate them and separate them, either live in desperate lonely separation or are pressed together into a mass."[14] The despair Arendt feels reflects the loss of history and the attendant loss of freedom that consumes the heart of liberal thought today.

[13] *Ibid.*, pp. 86, 87.
[14] *Ibid.*, pp. 89-90.

2

The Dilemma of the Social Critics

It is not . . . the waning of faith in reason among the intellectuals and the political thinkers of the English-speaking world which perturbs me most, but the loss of the pervading sense of a world in perpetual motion. This seems at first sight paradoxical; for rarely has so much superficial talk been heard of changes going on around us. But the significant thing is that change is no longer thought of as achievement, as opportunity, as progress, but as an object of fear. . . . Good historians . . . have the future in their bones. Beside the question: Why? the historian also asks the question: Whither?

E. H. CARR*

The writings of the social critics are eloquent testimony of the loss of history, because fundamental to their criticism of contemporary American society is their inability to create new and alternate forms of social activity. The society they describe is one cut off from the past. Implicit in their works is the necessity for the evolution of a new idea of freedom, one that instigates change as a means of self-transcendence. At the same time their description of society is, by its very nature, one that cannot make a history. Man in this society is bound to the present social system indefinitely; he can only imitate and repeat what he feels the collective judgments of himself should be.

The social critics can be faulted on the grounds that they are not always conscious of the meaning of history either within the context of their own thought or within the larger framework of society. In fact, they often display a surprising

* E. H. Carr, *What Is History?* (New York: Alfred A. Knopf, 1962).

naïveté; Riesman's and Mills's attempts to develop a historical context for their theories are symptomatic, as shall be seen later. But their failure in historical interpretation is not to the point; it is not the source of their history-less condition. The source is the picture they present of American society as one which achieves a static condition purified of change. All their thrusts against American society, all the theories about other-directed men, power elites, organization men, growing up absurd, and many others, come to the point of proving that this society is one which does not have the dynamics of history within it.[1]

Indeed, they prove it only too well. They not only show how this society shuts off the future-as-change, but in doing so they perforce imply that the hope for freedom is destroyed. Given the type of society they describe, the only real hope for freedom must lie in the future. The dilemma and irony of the social critic is that more than anyone else in his society he sees the need for history, for change, the need to get out of this society through historical development, but having proved that our society has no operating principle other than that of the squirrel cage of other-direction, that it has no principle or force of self-transcendence, he is stuck in the circle of his proof.

If no one is more aware than the social critic of the need for history-as-change, no one is less able to see it as a real possibility.

The Dilemma of The Other

The problem of history which the social critic must meet is made manifest by and underlines the seminal ideas and con-

[1] For a work that is sensitively aware of what the author calls the withdrawal "from history, from politics, from the ideology of culture," and the "pietistic quietism" of our time, see Richard Chase, *The Democratic Vista* (Doubleday and Company, 1958).

cepts of David Riesman in *The Lonely Crowd.* There the history of change from the tradition-directed individual (who accepts unquestionably the lore of his tribe) through the inner-directed (who derives his cause for action from a set of internalized values) to the other-directed (who takes his cue from "a jury of his peers") is in essence a history of freedom. Riesman specifically warns against the identification of inner-direction with freedom, but the burden of his work suggests that the other-directed intrinsically lacks the ability to innovate. He describes "the other-directed round of life" as one of "the glad hand," "manipulative skills," "fair trade," "expense accounts," and "entertainment as group adjustment." The other-directed handles his environment, but since he seeks the approval of The Other, he does not have autonomy.

Politics have become so impregnated with other-direction that it now consists of nothing more than veto groups, capable only of blocking one another rather than providing a creative dynamic. Politics, therefore, ceases to be the means by which man and society transcend themselves. The "inside-dopesters" dominate the field.

Riesman concludes this truly significant analysis, perhaps the most searching work on America and Americans since World War II, with a discussion of autonomy as contrasted with the adjustment ethos of the inner-directed. Autonomy, he makes clear, is not to be identified with inner-direction, but with the ability of choosing whether or not to conform. Autonomy is an achievement beyond the ordinary in our society. "False personalization," "enforced privatization," and "the problem of competence"—all destroy the possibilities of autonomy. What is most significant in the America of today is Riesman's identification of freedom with autonomy and only autonomy.

The other-directed character dominant today creates a situation that forces Riesman to see society in terms so new that the old categories no longer fit. For example, in place of Marx's class struggle he invents a characterological struggle. But, unlike Marx, Riesman has no firm belief in history; he can find no reason to believe that a society of the autonomous is coming into being or even can come into being. The contrast with the proletariat could not be stronger. The missing ingredient is a faith in the onward forces of history.

Riesman's other-directed character is by definition an ahistorical fellow. In the eyes of the other-directed, the issues of his society take on none of the qualities of an encounter in history, but, because he is what he is, of an encounter only of position, role, or status in his present society, the only society he can conceive. The characterological struggle is about the domination of new modes of conformity. "The struggle of classes and societies may . . . be viewed, to some extent, as a struggle among different characterological adaptations to the situation created by the dominance of a given mode of insuring conformity."[2] More simply, it is about the gradual succession of the three characters—the inner-directed, the other-directed, and the autonomous—to dominance. But such statements hide the most significant aspect of this struggle, which is that the other-directed, as distinct from the inner-directed, has no concept of the historical significance of his struggle, or, to be more exact, no concept of history. And he cannot have such a concept because he is not directed toward anything but what his fellowmen expect of him.[3] History, after all, must be going someplace or there is no story to it and

[2] David Riesman, Reuel Denney, and Nathan Glazer, *The Lonely Crowd* (New Haven, Conn.: Yale University Press, 1950), p. 31. Hereafter cited, with all respect to Denney and Glazer, as Riesman, *The Lonely Crowd*.

[3] Ralf Dahrendorf in *Culture and Social Character: the Work of David Riesman Reviewed*, ed. Seymour Martin Lipset and Leo Lowenthal (New York: The Free Press of Glencoe, 1961), p. 196, makes a similar point when he says: "Perfect other-direction means that history has come to a standstill."

it signifies nothing. But the other-directed is not the person even to contemplate such a problem, let alone do anything about it. His forte is to adjust, not to create or lead. A nation of other-directed people would be an awesome sight, each of them peering anxiously at the others to see what he should do next. Such a nation may never exist in fact, but insofar as the other-directed is the predominant type within a society then such a history-less drift would take hold. The other-directed is the loss of history made manifest in individual character.

The ahistorical qualities of the other-directed have led for the first time in modern history to a dominant character whose fundamental project is to be outside of history. This fact alone is of revolutionary consequence as far as a view of our history is concerned. Riesman himself postulates that the coming amongst us and the arrival at dominance of the other-directed is one of the great and fundamentally revolutionary changes in Western civilization. The immense significance of the other-directed is based specifically on the belief and assumption that this shift is the second shift of such magnitude, the first being the shift from traditional to inner-directed man.

Thus what has occurred to us today is not uniqueness derived from a historical evolution but uniqueness springing from revolutionary change. Such distinctive uniqueness involves Riesman—and those who have adopted his methods—in the use of new terminologies and new sociological concepts to describe the era in which we live. What is important here, however, is not method but the quality of our time as he sees it and its separateness from the long period that came before it. We are now, according to this view, involved in a revolutionary break with our past in which the problems and solutions of inner-directed man have nothing to tell the other-directed even if he were interested—which he is not.

Thus Riesman separates us from the past by telling us that we are not continuing a story but beginning a new one. It is a story in which politics provides no fulcrum for change. His concept of "veto politics" and of dispersed power is one characterized by ceaseless movement rather than significant and purposeful change. Politics was once an engine for change, an engine by means of which power hierarchies pursued their will and achieved what they wanted. Today it is passive; no one pursues anything, and nothing is achieved. Indeed, if one is to wait for politics to produce the future, there will be no future except continuation. History will have become not a story but a broken record. Thus the idea of a history and politics are separated. For Riesman politics becomes a recreational sport. Occasionally he drops a remark in *The Lonely Crowd* that suggests the importance of political commitment; but politics in his view is simply one way among others to strengthen the psyche rather than a way to effect social change. For example, he sees engagement in marginal political groups as mainly valuable for its psychological benefit to the individual and offers little consideration of any possible political and social impact it may possess.

Where, then, shall we look for the future? Riesman, who is aware of this problem, finds an answer in the autonomous person. Individual autonomy must give the clue to the future and must make history if any is to be made. For by definition the other-directed, the predominant character type of our time, cannot make history. He can only repeat history. But no one, and certainly not Riesman, who invented him, expects him to put society onto a historical track. History-making potential can only lie with the autonomous. But Riesman's very concept of the nature of such men negates any hope that they will take up the burden abandoned so willingly by the other-directed. For the autonomous man is defined by Riesman as one who is "free to choose whether to conform or not."[4]

Can we expect such a man to move history? Manifestly not,

---

[4] See Riesman, *The Lonely Crowd,* chap. 12.

since his preoccupation and, more important, his only dis-
tinguishing characteristic, the thing that marks him off from
the other-directed, is merely an ability to choose between
what already exists. He is, as distinct from the other-directed,
capable of choosing whether to join this group or that,
whether to conform, whether to associate himself with the
society that exists or to withdraw from it. But he is not in any
way a man who will decide and show through action that
history is the development of alternative ways of existence.
Nor does Riesman seem to believe that such is or would be
the case, for his main object in putting autonomous man forward as the solution to the dilemmas of the time is simply to
preserve what little freedom is possible in this day and age
against the other-directed.[5] Riesman sees freedom today as
being in desperate straits. And such being the case, the best
he can hope for is what might be called a desperate freedom,
one which might be preserved by the ability of autonomous
man to say No! But that is all.

Autonomous man is an offshoot of other-directed man and
shares his doubts. He is more concerned with looking over his
shoulder to see what The Other is doing behind his back
than he is in looking forward to see how he might be able to
create new social forms. He is, alas, the disapproving and
maverick brother of other-directed man.

Riesman holds out some hope. He believes that the dis-
parity between social character and social structure, which is
responsible for the characterological struggle, will bring
about social change as distinct from personal freedom. But he
never comes to the point of telling how the mechanism is supposed to work. And for a good reason. The autonomous man
has a vested interest in fending off threats to his personal

---

[5] It should be made clear that Riesman sees virtues in the other-directed
that offer the possibility of movement toward autonomy.

freedom and in finding a role and place for autonomy in the present society, rather than in finding and making a different society. Personal freedom as opposed to engagement in the processes of social change becomes an end in itself.

The autonomous man, at his best, will turn to politics under non-crisis conditions (hardly the most fruitful time in terms of history-making), with motives that are neither moralistic nor group-conforming, simply because of the interest he may find in politics, because politics would be a way of helping himself to understand his world.[6]

This picture of a slightly baffled autonomous man going in for politics in order to understand the world about him does not incline one to believe that the future as history will be made by him. Riesman can only offer us hope—no scheme, no framework for historical change—when he says that autonomous man will become a social force by showing how life can be lived with vitality and happiness.[7]

Although the above strictures are accurate, they are too harsh; Riesman, in the very act of putting forward the idea of and hope for autonomy in an other-directed world, has at least made it possible to hope for an open future and one that therefore may have a history. It is a real and significant achievement. For if some freedom, even a desperate, defensive freedom, can be maintained in the face of the other-directed, then history is possible, because with free men anything is possible. Autonomy may be the last and ultimate way of preserving the possibility of a future history in an era when nothing else but the preservation of possibility is feasible. But we must say that if this situation is the one that in fact obtains, then freedom is indeed a desperate thing and is reduced

[6] Riesman, *The Lonely Crowd*, pp. 370-371.
[7] *Ibid.*, p. 120.

to its minimum. Instead of being used to make a future, it is used only to mark time.

Thus Riesman, who is more painfully and clearly aware of the need for change and the need for history to be moved in the direction of freedom than most of us, must end his *The Lonely Crowd* with a utopia. It is a significant note for him to strike, and one which indicates the failure of autonomous man as a historical force. For it is precisely the characteristic of a utopia to be outside of history. It is outside history for two reasons. First, it is the answer of those who dislike the trend of events and who cannot see any other historical trend in sight to counter the unpleasant future they see before them. In this sense utopian thinking is not so much ahistorical as antihistorical. Second, it is a postulate of a future that depends for its achievement on a leap out of present historical reality, a leap that can only be achieved by a "moral" or "intellectual" conversion, a conversion that will repudiate and confound the known facts of history.[8] Both aspects of utopian thinking are found in Riesman's final essay in *The Lonely Crowd* as he faces the historical feebleness of our society. He asks if the other-directed will wake up to the fact that they overconform. His answer is that it is "exceedingly unlikely." Nevertheless he claims that there is the hope that people in their private lives may be constantly nurturing new standards, that they may discover what is wrong and become more attentive to their own feelings and standards.[9] One may agree that they may do so, but also claim that such possibilities ignore and bypass the problems of history and society.

None of this is to deny the importance of utopian thinking —as Riesman nobly says, the one thing we can no longer

[8] For an excellent critique of Erich Fromm's position in this respect see John H. Schaar, *Escape from Authority, the Perspectives of Erich Fromm* (New York: Basic Books, Inc., 1961).

[9] *Ibid.*, chap. 18.

afford is the luxury of non-utopian thought. But what is so striking about *The Lonely Crowd* when considered in relationship to the problem of history is that its acute analysis of American society portrays myriad forces that are crushing and will continue to crush freedom. Working in its favor are only the feeblest of forces—if autonomous man can be called a force. Those forces working against freedom are the actual concrete historical realities of our time for which autonomous man has no answer. Autonomous man is depressing. He is better off in a graduate school, where most of them end up anyway.

What has been said here of Riesman's *The Lonely Crowd* can also be said of a quite different approach. Though *The Lonely Crowd* and C. Wright Mills's *The Power Elite* clash on some important concepts, they meet on the common ground of their inability to cope with history, an inability, needless to say, that is the result not of intellectual failure but of the particular way they see society. In their approach to society, where there was history there is now a blank space.

The Self-Closing Trap

If Riesman sees us in a desperate situation and tries to find a way out, C. Wright Mills in his most important criticism of American society, *The Power Elite,* presents us with a dilemma so absolute and total that history comes to a dead stop with a thump and a thud. Obviously there is no recipe for facing the problems of retreat from the situation that is feared. Obviously too, some indication of the historical forces at work would help resolve a situation that will kill freedom if it continues.

Mills's view of society is based on a dichotomy between a mass of individuals who have lost control of their own lives

and an elite who command the big organizations and make
the big decisions. The elite is economic, political, and military, and is composed of those who know each other and, as
Mills says, "take one another into account." It decides national events, it is the Big They, the ambiguous agents of
decision. They are found among the very rich, among the
military hierarchy, and among those whom Mills calls "the political directorate." He no longer believes that society in America is balanced in accordance with Riesman's veto groups.
Instead of a society in which no one does anything, there is a
small group that supposedly does everything. The rigidity of
the situation is its hallmark; the flaccidity of the mass society
under the control of the power elite allows no opportunity
for groups or individuals to undermine the power elite. No
change can occur in the basic structure in society. "The top
of modern American society is increasingly unified, and often
seems wilfully co-ordinated: at the top there has emerged an
elite of power. The middle levels are a drifting set of stale-
mated, balancing forces: the middle does not link the bottom
with the top. The bottom of this society is politically frag-
mented, and even as a passive fact, increasingly powerless: at
the bottom there is emerging a mass society."[10]

In his system, no freedom other than that which benefits the
power elite can prevail. Are we, then, trapped? So it would
seem, for Mills's analysis leads us to a dead end. Indeed, it
represents the self-closing trap found in much of liberal
thought today, a trap that is self-closing because the liberal has
lost his sense of historical change and development. All he can
prove with his finespun analyses is that the society in which
he lives will be the ruination of freedom. Mills is among the
most symptomatic of the social critics because he drives the
logic of his position to its conclusion.

[10] C. Wright Mills, *The Power Elite* (New York: Oxford University Press,
Inc., 1956), p. 324.

In part this self-closing tendency comes from an inability to show the historical process by which we arrived at our present state. And, not being able to show how we got where we are, there is no historical continuum which might give us some insight as to how we might get someplace else. To be sure, he mentions that the means of producing and exploiting violence have been progressively enlarged and centralized in a "fairly straight line,"[11] but such statements are hardly a theory of past history and certainly give us no clear explanation of why and how we have come to have the power elite foisted on us today. Nor, in fact, does Riesman's belief that character types correspond to population shifts seem either plausible or helpful. It, too, has the inadequacies of all single-factor approaches to history. Further, both approaches—they can hardly be called theories of history—have the weakness of not demonstrating mechanisms of change. They simply correlate the existence of events occurring simultaneously in time. Simple correlations may provide a clue for the research worker, but the actual task is to show what the methods of change and development have been. Marx, among others, clearly recognized that necessity; simple correlations interested him very little. But, correlations or not, Mills has little use for history; as he says, we learn that we cannot learn from history.[12]

He does not, however, quite live up to his precept, for there is one lesson he has learned and that is that liberalism is down to its last whimper. One of the main characteristics of our time is found in the complete break between liberalism and the facts of life today. Consequently, liberalism, according to Mills, cannot exist any longer as an effective force; conflict between liberalism and the power elite is shadow-boxing. The past of a significant liberal conflict with the ruling elite is as

[11] *Ibid.*, p. 22.
[12] *Ibid.*

dead as a dodo, and as relevant. What the liberal once possessed as a set of beliefs and ideas now has become simply a means of masking reality. For the liberal in particular, in Mills's view, the break between past and present is complete. Once he might have been able to assume a conflict between himself and the power elite, but he cannot do so anymore. The power elite has won.

So important is it for Mills to postulate and formulate the idea of this break, this particular and significant rip in the fabric of American life, that it is one of the main objects of his *The Power Elite* to establish its reality. And it is precisely because of the intellectual and political collapse of American liberalism and its weakness as a political theory in the face of the facts of today that our era is not simply unique in the usual historical sense, but what might be called totally unique, so different as to have destroyed continuity with the past. The power elite has been growing among us for some time; it is necessary once more to recall that "fairly straight line." But with the collapse of liberalism the giant has become full-grown and it stands on its own two feet. The question of how to live with it will not be found in the past exactly because the past failed to prevent the giant from becoming Gargantuan. The past has failed to provide us with solutions and must, therefore, be banished from our thinking today.

Such is the basic assumption of Mills in his *The Power Elite*, and the source of his own peculiar form of loss of history. But having lost the past in the midst of our totally unique society, what of the future? Will this new society create equally new forms of conflict that will overcome the power elite and provide a new source of freedom now that the old source of change—liberalism—has gone? Not according to Mills. He places us in a new and decidedly unpleasant society with no exit. From his own evidence, the power elite is so dominant, so all-powerful, and so assured of its continued growth that the possibility of a different development is negated at the very start of his discussion. As he puts it, the power elite has robbed politics of any alternatives except those of the elite itself.[13]

We have seen in the case of Riesman how opaque the future has become in terms of change. The same is true for Mills. Despite his later efforts to fight his way out of the self-closing trap, his pessimism and his blindness to anything but the present is even more complete because he postulates that the "fairly straight line" of development of the power elite has not yet reached its apex (if it ever will; we are not informed on that question). Thus the worst is yet to come. Nor can we, he tells us glumly, take any comfort from the ups and downs of elites in earlier periods; for evidently the straight line is losing whatever kinks it once had and thus has become more inexorable. Our elite is here to stay. Thus we have no place to go but up or down, depending, perhaps, on which way one is looking at the straight line.

If the elite dominates us as completely as Mills claims, and if there are no alternatives to it, then it follows that the future will not be a place of history-as-change, but of repetition. He does not even discuss the possibility of revolution; indeed the word does not even appear in the table of contents. This is no world of revolution. This is an age of doldrums.

But the total blankness of the future is not simply the result of his empirical assumption that opposition to the power elite is not likely. It is also the result of the inner logic of the power elite itself as he presents it to us. He tells us that "although we are all of us within history we do not all possess equal powers to make history,"[14] by which he means that if the

[13] *Ibid.*, p. 274.
[14] *Ibid.*, p. 22.

masses cannot affect the future the power elite can. But can the power elite affect history? After consideration of the situation described by Mills, a situation in which the power elite rides high, wide, and handsome, how is it possible to say that such an elite either can or will affect history in any fundamental sense? Is it not, on the contrary, more accurate to say that, along with the rest of us, it too is trapped in the same static existence? Indeed, the lesson that one takes away from Mills's powerful and sometimes convincing indictment of our society is that no one—no one at all—will make history, that the power elite, like the rest of us poor fools, has lost history too. And for two reasons: first, if it tries to change history in any significant sense it will undermine its own power and destroy its very being as a power elite. It has, after all, arrived; the logic of its position is not to change but to fix society as it is; and one may expect with confidence that it will devote all its dominant and crushing talents to that effort. Its existence and its whole being form the absolute necessity from its own point of view—and who else's point of view will be considered?—of bringing history to a stop. History as the story of change may or may not be made in the future, but it will not be because of anything done by the power elite who will rest satisfied and assured if it sells its quota of goods and television trash each and every day. The power elite as history makers? It is even less likely to change history than the rest of us, for it has everything to lose if there is change, while the rest of us might possibly gain if its power was divided and the elite itself were chivvied into extinction.

Secondly, it is not simply the logic of self-survival, on Mills's own showing, that would prevent the power elite we now have from bringing about change. It is its positive incapacity to contemplate or even conceive of that innovation which is the essence of change. Mills himself says that the men of power today are not so much dogmatic as mindless,[15] and if such is the case their ability to effect change of any significance, to get us out, so to speak, of the age of the power elite, is, of necessity, nil.

This conclusion relates to the central weakness of Mills's work: its inability to demonstrate what the power elite does with its power. The thread of mystery throughout his book is the puzzling lack of concrete description about the actual activity of the power elite. We are told it exists; we are told of whom it is composed. But we never see it in action. Eventually the thought strikes the reader that perhaps it doesn't act, that it simply exists, that it aims not to act and that it is incapable of action (other, of course, than the physical act of making, buying, and selling goods). If such is the case—and the evidence of Mills's book and everything we know about the power elite from other experience indicates that it is— then we are faced with the startling but depressing conclusion that the very significance of the power elite, its very threat, is its inability to make history, to instigate change, to drive us on to new things, new ways of living and thinking. Stuck we are, and this time for good, on the treadmill of meaninglessness.[16]

It is to be hoped that Mills's description of the domination of the power elite is not entirely correct. But insofar as it is correct we are in the presence of a Leviathan that gives us no anticipation of moving into an era in which a new kind

[15] *Ibid.*, p. 356.

[16] That C. Wright Mills was aware of and concerned about the problem of history that has been presented here is demonstrated by his *The Sociological Imagination* (New York: Oxford University Press, Inc., 1959), especially by chapter 8, "The Uses of History." That he was unable to "use" history to dissolve the dilemma that he presented in *The Power Elite* is also demonstrated by *The Sociological Imagination*, especially by chapter 10, "On Politics." The same fissure—a fissure between values and reality—that is found in Mills's thought in this respect, is also found in Riesman's.

of freedom can exist. The power elite is not, by definition, interested in a new kind of society, and even if it were, it is too stupid to do anything about it. It is not interested in anything except power, money, and survival—hardly the characteristics of a dynamic maker of history, unless the observer can show counterforces working within or against it, which, as we have seen, Mills cannot.

The writings of Riesman and Mills may engage the question of history obliquely, but they cannot avoid it. They must indicate a position since both are manifestly concerned with an interpretation of our society as a whole; the substantial ghost of history stalks through their pages, whether they wish it or not. And the same is true of other social critics, those who aim to present partial theories of our ills and to illuminate simply one aspect of our society.

To carry this interrogation into the realm of the partial theorists it will be sufficient to look at the writings of John Kenneth Galbraith and Paul Goodman in order to see the problems of living as a liberal without history. Both have attempted—with some success—to move liberalism off its defensive stance. Both have attempted to show how liberalism is relevant to this age as a critique of its senselessness, its "conventional wisdom" or its "absurdity." In their attempt to move society forward to more rational grounds and away from the absurdity and conventional wisdom that rule our time, what help do they expect from history?

In an Affluent Limbo

Both Galbraith and Goodman, the one in *The Affluent Society*, the other in *Growing Up Absurd*, see our situation as one in which new forces are at work in what is necessarily a new society. American capitalism in *The Affluent Society* is not the previous capitalistic system writ large but a new capitalistic system in which the old rules no longer apply. The whole burden of this book is that conventional wisdom is conventional, certainly; but no longer wisdom.[17] Galbraith sees a seamless web spun out from the industrial revolution up to the present. The break with history comes with the affluence of our American society. The old rules were operative so long as there was a common set of experiences applicable to a society in which the fundamental economic fact was scarcity. From Adam Smith and David Ricardo to World War II there was no significant break in economic thought because, according to Galbraith, all economic theorists, including Marx, were concerned with the allocation of scarce goods. But now new rules for behavior become necessary. Newness is the essential fact to grasp.

The decisive change occurs in our time; the earlier period, the 150 years previous, is seen as a whole. One consistent train of thought was real, successful (within its own assumptions), and relevant. Change occurred within that period, but it was contained within the operative system of ideas that characterized the whole period. Now, however, all is different. Now those thoughts, ideas, and concepts of the earlier age are museum pieces, telling us how our ancestors once thought, but affording us no guidance or help in our problems today. Quite the contrary, they are a positive hindrance. The crucial fact of affluence has made a dustbin of all history. It is something the world has never seen before. Without engaging in dramatics, the calm and quiet voice of Galbraith brings us the chilling message that we are setting in motion new forces in history. Not since the eighteenth century have economic relationships undergone such a change. The roots may have

[17] One of Galbraith's complaints, of course, about conventional wisdom is that it perpetuates an irrelevant past in the new present.

come into being in the past; the flower is a new phonomenon. Galbraith creates the idea not merely of change but of our profound and deep break with the past. Thus he establishes the fact that history as the story of what happened before our times holds little or no importance for us as we face the problems of our uniqueness.

Paul Goodman, taking a different tack, comes to much the same point of view about the loss of our past. *Growing Up Absurd* tells the story of "Youth in the Organized System." However, a more general critique is presented in which the central focus is on the absurdity (the senselessness and meaninglessness) of our social actions. In brief, we became absurd because of what he calls our "missed revolutions." They were the chances we once had (mainly in the 1930's) for that basic, fundamental, and revolutionary change that could have reoriented our society toward worthwhile ends. We have inherited this failure, this lack. As he says, "History is especially significant when those lost causes haunt us in the present as unfinished business."[18]

History has now become the story of what failed to happen rather than the story of what actually happened. The revolution that never came to be has the effect of disrupting tradition without achieving a new "social balance." The revolution that "half-occurs," that is "compromised," that is never carried through, brings about social change in some areas and fails to do this in other areas. Technology and efficiency have revolutionized the production of goods, but the privilege of managing has not been taken away from the businessman. "The actual results have been slums of . . . engineering." Another example, drawn from the New Deal, shows that government ". . . has cushioned the business cycle and maintained nearly full employment . . ." but has not ". . . achieved

18 Paul Goodman, *Growing Up Absurd* (New York: Random House, Inc., 1960), p. 216.

its ideal social balance between public and private works."[19] We exist today with the depressing effects of the aborted revolutions all around us. "Tradition has been broken, yet there is no new standard to affirm. . . . A missed revolution makes irrelevant the community that persists. And a compromised revolution tends to shatter the community that was, without an adequate substitute."[20] In short, we are in limbo.

The image Goodman has of our lack of historical situation is fundamentally that of the other critics we have considered, but with the distinctive quality of making us aware that our break with the past has had disastrous consequences. For Goodman claims that the past is important since it is no longer operative—an original claim, for it attempts to save the past for radicalism. Instead of saying that the past must be rejected because it has failed, he says that it must be adopted, must be reintegrated with the present. For some, such an attempt represents old-fashioned radicalism. Comments like these are not only snide; they miss the point of his attitude toward the past. He sees the gap we are in, but tells us that the past can have a revolutionary significance. He is one of the very few to give us this news—and it is news—and one may only regret that he has not developed more fully this insight.[21] Liberalism has been deprived of its historical roots in this society. When Goodman talks about the missed and compromised revolutions of the past, he is talking about the need for the idea of a history. Those who whine about the emptiness of old-fashioned radicalism create the predicament from which he tries to extract us.

Goodman finds that the past in general does have a use and that for our society it can have a use. But he also knows that

[19] *Ibid.*, pp. 218-219.
[20] *Ibid.*, p. 217.
[21] He does list in one chapter the measures that have failed and that could be reinvigorated today for revolutionary purposes, but listing is not a discussion.

for our times history is not operative in fact by virtue of our missing and abortive revolutions. For Goodman the past should be useful but it is not. Consequently we are stuck with a loss of history. Without history we become, literally, absurd.

Goodman's presentation of the cutting of our historical roots leaves him in the company of the melancholy crew of social critics. What grounds do we have for hoping that the missed and compromised revolutions will be taken up? The question receives a thundering silence as an answer. New forces may not exist, but if they do exist, they have not yet been discovered or described.

If Goodman's view of the future can be characterized as optimism suspended in mid-air, what of Galbraith's vision of the future? As we have seen, he finds even more of a caesura dividing our time from time past. Given his liberal aims, hopes, and schemes for the ills of the Affluent Society, does he and can he postulate any way in which a new history will put his solutions into effect? In answering that question we come across a curious contradiction in his thought indicative of the difficulty of finding grounds for a belief in history.

The contradiction appears when *The Affluent Society* is compared to Galbraith's earlier *American Capitalism*. In its analysis of the American economy this work makes certain assumptions about history that are lacking in *The Affluent Society*. Instead of the sharp attack on the "conventional wisdom" of the past and a hypothesis about the uniqueness of an Affluent Society, *American Capitalism* postulates that our present economic system—still subsumed under the nomenclature of capitalism—is simply another and highly developed form of our past capitalistic system. Galbraith's view requires a new theory to understand the operation and development of capitalism, but a theory that does not depart from the canons of capitalism itself. To find relief from its stresses and strains he offers his idea of countervailing power—an only slightly curdled variety of the pure milk of classical economics. The tension that obtains between large organizations within the already established system—the A & P or CIO, for example—is made fruitful by pitting one against the other. The basic power structure of American capitalism is not disturbed, but is made more secure, more serviceable in its own terms. It is, so to speak, the laissez-faire creed of the supermarkets.

More important, *American Capitalism* is firmly anchored in the past; the present variety of capitalism is simply an off-shoot of the main trunk. America has a future consisting of a bigger and more sophisticated capitalism. There is no loss of history in this work; quite the contrary, history past, present, and future is seen not as problematical and dubious, but assured. History will continue to develop capitalism in America. One can fairly hear the capitalistic system ringing down the grooves of time.

Quite different is the approach of *The Affluent Society*. Here Galbraith describes not only the new society based on affluence, but tells us that it is necessary to find some other form of social organization to replace its absurdities, that we must move and change in the future in order to discover different ways of living. But does he offer any reason to believe that we will be able to move away from the Affluent Society into something more rational? It is true that he does offer solutions like enforced retirement, reduction of the workweek, and investment in education. But we must ask: what reason do we have to believe that the solutions he offers will be realized? The answer is, very little. To work against the new force of history, to sweep away the trash of private capitalism which is ruining the country, government must not be simply a countervailing force, but become a dominant force. His claim is audacious in the extreme. The very audacity of his idea indicates the depth of his belief that we have witnessed a break with our history and must move into a future different from the present.

Yet it is audacity in a historical vacuum. In Galbraith's analysis of the Affluent Society he fails to show that there are historical counterefforts that will produce the changes required. Nor does he discuss the political possibilities for realizing such solutions. Unless evidence to the contrary is suggested, the history of such a society must inevitably be to obey the logic of conspicuous production until it breaks down. No evidence of change in the system is in fact suggested by Galbraith, and there is no sign of any significant breakdown.

One may say further that, unless some historical force is operating to change society, Galbraith's procedures and solutions will only aid the continued growth and solidity of the present power structure. They may indeed modify the Affluent Society as it is now constituted; they may and probably will make it more livable, less overtly crazy than it is today; but it is doubtful indeed if they will do anything else. To have confidence that the Affluent Society will be changed significantly in the future, it is necessary to have a concept of historical change that will give us some belief at least that change will occur or can occur, that the issue is still open.[22]

The Cost of Losing History

The liberal social critic today has told us that our society is No Good. He tells us that it should be changed. The rest is silence.

[22] Other works of the social critics could be discussed to the same effect. Thus William Whyte's *The Organization Man,* although based on an appreciation of the historical changes in social ideas that have led up to the present ideology of social ethics, nevertheless displays the same inability to postulate a future of change, the same inability to see any alternative form of existence developing out of our present existence. Indeed, the iron grasp of the present

The liberal pays a mortal price for allowing himself to be stuck in the present. For him there is no continuity between past and present and no line thrown out to the future. The philosophical cost is reflected in the pessimism so characteristic of the social critic of today. And there is what might be called a political cost in his impotence as he views with distaste the life he and others must live.

The pessimism results from the loss of any reason for the belief that society will improve in the direction of freedom or that change will in any way manifest itself. Society seems to be fixed and complete in its fundamentals and will career through time like a stone, passing by a variety of objects, but in itself lacking the ability to absorb new forms of behavior from its environment. Society's present immobility is the ground bass of liberal social criticism today. The rhythm of the future is the beat of the present. No doubt there may be some surprises in store, but they do not appear on the horizon; they have given no indication of their existence; they exist only as an abstract possibility without real content. What other kind of society is possible for us? The loss of history makes the question impossible to answer.

This pessimism is not just a drastic reversal of eighteenth- and nineteenth-century beliefs that freedom would broaden from precedent down to precedent. It strikes at the very belief in freedom itself, for if one assumes, as do the social critics, that freedom is in a bad way in our society, that the forces that threaten it are potent and growing, and that it is impossible to see any force working in its favor, then it is hardly possible to believe that there is a future for freedom. No doubt some

---

is even more intense in the work of Whyte, for instead of seeing a break between our past and present he sees the present as a logical culmination of a history that has stopped producing anything new. In his case it might be said that there is not so much a loss of history as there is an end or a stop to history; in his scheme history produced the organization man and then came to a halt.

fragments may be saved from the ruins, but even they will have to be guarded carefully since they are under direct siege. It becomes difficult to search for freedom when the assumption is made that the search will be fruitless. The very definition of the word takes on an increasingly static meaning, since it can only be defined in terms of the defense of what is instead of what will be. Let us hold on, they say, to what we have, and we will have done well. Thoughts on the subject of freedom become immobilized when they become pessimistic through the loss of history.

In such a condition the conservative has a great advantage over the liberal, for the former lives in the myth of a fixed and happy past. He can turn back to that past and hence ignore the reality in which he lives. The conservative likes things that are dead because they are safe; he flourishes in an era of the loss of history because change upsets him, and he hopes to avoid it.[23] The liberal, on the other hand, aims to live with change because whatever else freedom is, it must first be the willingness to experiment through change. He withers in the pessimism that can see no promise but repetition.

Hence the political cost of the loss of history. The word "political" here does not mean only participation in but a belief and interest in the importance and validity of the political process. The political arena is the place where decisions for change should be made and where traditionally they have been made. But what happens to the political realm in the eyes of the liberal when he has lost his sense of history? He can no longer see it as the means by which society is driven forward and by which new forms of freedom can be created. Therefore his sense of politics, his belief and interest in

----

[23] An example of Madison Avenue's approach to history is not without interest. An advertisement of the Television Information Office is entitled "How to Discover the Past in a Brave New World." The answer, among others, is to watch David Brinkley! (*The Reporter,* January 4, 1962.)

politics, atrophies. Instead of seeing himself and others as participants in a political adventure, he sees himself and others as drudges in a wearisome round of repetitious, petty, and uninteresting—because unimportant—political maneuvers.

Such politics may have a certain significance because they may defend what freedom still exists, e.g. the politics of anti-McCarthyism. And it may be of some academic interest to observe what is not done in certain political maneuverings, what the failures have been. But fundamentally such politics is dull because it does not address itself to the problem of freedom, does not create significant alternatives to what exists. Can politics touch and work on the problem of defining alternatives? Whatever its abstract possibilities, in the eyes of the social critics it does not. It ceases to be the place where the future-as-change is born and becomes the place where the future-as-repetition is continued. The political cost of the loss of history is a loss of the idea of politics as the arena in which historical forces are at work to create a future different from the present. Politics swings from a concern with trivia to panic in the face of nuclear dangers.

The existentialist leap provides an answer to those who are pessimistic, but reliance on such a leap is evidence of despair. Intellectual belief in the possibility of rational, willed, and controlled change collapses. The existentialist postulates are a-intellectual and cannot therefore have any significant role in a study of political thought that tries to establish reasons for action. We can only note its prevalence today as a symptom. Another way of achieving change is by a theory of change, a concept of how certain changes can come about, or will come about, and a description of what is making or will make them come about. Such a theory need not be, of course, deterministic, but one that discerns certain possibilities and/-or probabilities for change as they exist in the present situation. A theory of change is required if the threats to freedom described by the social critics of our time are to be resolved, but those very threats themselves have been responsible for the loss of any history that could produce such a theory. Stuck in the present, our critics are also stuck on the horns of this dilemma.

The loss of history is not entirely without advantage for the liberal. It gives him freedom from a dead past if nothing else. But it can open the present to invention only if the present is conceived as a part of a historical process that will create a future. Because the liberal makes an identification between change and freedom, it is he who provides the forward drive in a society and who creates a historical continuum by his concept of what history is about. When he is unable to do so, not only does he lose his particular role but the whole society loses its quality of invention and spontaneity. The loss of history is a tragedy not only for the liberal but for the whole society.[24]

To put the issue in dramatic terms, if the liberal is to save America as well as himself, one of his first problems is to develop a historical approach to determine whether this particular era in which we live is one of fixity, or whether it is capable of change. If the latter, then it will be necessary to ask in what areas change is possible and by what means. The liberal as a social critic has done marvelously well in describing some of the basic features of our civilization. But the failure to deal with the problem of change in our society, to show how history is at work today, has meant the loss of one of the most significant weapons of liberal thought. Without it, without some concept of how to get out of what we are in, the liberal must confine his search for freedom to the present and to the society that he fears.

[24] It is worth pointing out that the anguished cries for national purpose today, insofar as they are sincere and not a merchandising technique, represent this general feeling among the public of having lost history, of having lost a sense of where we are going.

3

The Loss of Society

The last stage of the laboring society, the society of jobholders, demands of its members a sheer automatic functioning. . . . It is quite conceivable that the modern age—which began with such an unprecedented and promising outburst of human activity—may end in the deadliest, most sterile passivity history has ever known.

HANNAH ARENDT*

Faced with the loss of history there are those who say that such a loss is no bad thing, that we have had altogether too much history in this century. Considering the sum of anguish, tyranny, and terror that has characterized a considerable part of our past, it is not unnatural to conclude that it is better to try to live in one's own time, to make do with what exists, than to be overly concerned with history and the future. If the past was mainly disastrous and if there is nothing to look forward to, why not live in the here and now and derive from it whatever possibilities of freedom it may possess? It is a plausible, intriguing, and even comforting doctrine. But its viability depends on the quality and quantity of the possibilities which we see in the society in which we must live.

Given the loss of history as the ground bass of this attempt to live in the present, two alternatives present themselves to the liberal. He may look at his society and find it fundamentally good, find it enjoyable and something to be taken as

* Hannah Arendt, *The Human Condition* (Chicago: University of Chicago Press, 1958).

a gift of contingency which he has been fortunate enough to pick up. Or he may find it a threat to his most fundamental values. In that case he must discover some way to preserve freedom apart from society, some way to assert it against society. Then what happens to liberalism as a doctrine dedicated to the public concern? Is it possible to postulate freedom in a situation in which not only historical change works against it but in which society is actually hostile?

The problem posed by the attitudes of the social critics is that of the relationship of freedom to society. The search for freedom must take place within the context not only of historical but also of social concreteness and specificity. In one sense it is no more possible to lose society than it is to lose history, since a position must be taken on one as on the other. But it is possible to lose either or both the idea and hope that one's own society is the place where freedom may be found. The loss of society for the liberal can be said to signify the belief that it is acutely hostile to the individual rather than a place in which significant acts can and should occur, and which gives meaning and direction to human existence. It is a point of view that sees the social system as the provider of goods and services but with little or no significance beyond that role. Society as a supermarket, in this view, is conceived as achieving many important functions in the realm of economics and defense; but it is not conceived as touching the most important areas of life, which must therefore be left to private existence.[1]

---

[1] Obviously the loss of society involves many of the old problems of the relationship of the individual to society. But it includes much more than the old continuum of individual versus society. It carries with it a whole connotation of disgust, despair, and withdrawal from active participation. The old liberal individualist always found his venue within society; if nothing else it was necessary for his buccaneering raids, as the chicken coop, so to speak, that was necessary to his existence as individualist. Man against society was a dingdong battle and quite a joyous one in fact, for through it society provided

The Upper World of Bureaucratic Insolence and the Lower World of Insurgent Anarchy

Society as a supermarket, a cornucopia constantly supplying goods, is divided into two worlds, one being an upper world of bureaucratic power and the other a lower world of individual anarchy. In this situation a unit is split into two halves, neither of which can exist without the other but neither of which makes choice possible. The upper world allows no significant choice because it is only meaningless activity; the lower cannot create a meaningful activity because it lacks the attributes of form, structure, and institutions.

Freedom is not a meaningless activity nor is it simply the absence of restraint. Rather it is the ability to choose. But the ability to choose can only exist if there are some things that have value. An individual's personal life can give value to certain activities; hence freedom can exist in a private sphere. But an individual's social life can also give value to certain activities. In this sphere he can experience freedom because he can make a choice between one form of social activity or existence or another, because one form of social activity or existence has value to a greater or lesser extent. But society becomes absurd to him—becomes a cynical joke in which all crooks are equal—when it is composed of useless and uninteresting activities. Then his experiences in society are without value. He loses society.

A society divided into the two halves of bureaucratic insolence and individual anarchy is one that cannot be experienced as possessing value. The upper world is conceived as

the opposition and challenge and friction that made possible the growth and even the creation of an individual. (One has only to read in the nineteenth-century autobiography to be aware of this.) There was no withdrawal; instead there was a plunge into society and a sense of social adventure. The loss of society today is something quite different.

engaged in a meaningless game of moving counters from one
place to another, a game that feeds on itself and that leads to
nothing but more bureaucratic insolence. Society on this level
is without value because the bureaucratic game in and of itself
is without value, is a means without any end. In the lower
world of insurgent anarchy, on the other hand, freedom cannot be found, because anarchy is not freedom. Since social
anarchy is action without restraint the individual loses the
ability to choose between one thing and another; no criteria
of choice exist. Only where valued and active institutions
structure and inform the social order can the ability to choose
manifest itself. Institutions act as a discipline providing the
limits that distinguish between the concepts of freedom and
anarchy. Since institutions are the embodiment of social
value, their existence gives meaning and value, and hence
makes possible the ability to choose within society.

It is on this very issue that the puzzled liberal falls victim
to the conservative trap. The conservative cries, Anarchist!
The liberal trying to defend freedom often accepts the terms
of this argument. But in fact no one is more aware than he
that anarchy is precisely the rejection of structure, form, and
institutions, and hence the rejection of choice.

In a situation where the alternative to the upper world of
bureaucratic power is the lower world of insurgent anarchy,
society becomes meaningless, is lost. By virtue of the fact that
the lower world is unrestrained in its actions, and rejects the
institutions of society, the liberal who accedes to this world is
as equally without freedom as the insolent bureaucrat lost in
the hopeless round of organizational play. Indeed, both
groups are engaged in social play, which precludes choice in
society.

For those who see society in this way the search for freedom
manifestly can take place only within the structure founded

on one's personal existence. Objects of value determined by the individual in his private round and contrasted with social objects of no value, offer him a range of choice. Within narrow confines there is freedom but it is a personal, idiosyncratic freedom, which will prove to be what its opponents say it is, meaningless as a social phenomenon.

John Locke faced the problem of freedom and society in his own way and for his own time when he took man out of the formless flux of the state of nature and put him into the order of a social contract. But what was satisfactory for him as a solution is without content for us. We are faced with this old dilemma as if nothing had been said on the question, a question more pressing, more dangerous for us than for John Locke and those who followed him. They had a traditional system to rely on to carry them over the rough spots in their reasoning, but we have nothing but a plunging society, imbued with an aimlessness that seems sometimes suicidal and always frightening. In these circumstances a formless freedom, or, to use the excellent old term, a state of nature, is more possible today than ever before and more devastating in its impact. We are not going to settle this question of form and freedom once and for all, but we are going to solve it for our epoch or literally watch our freedom perish.

In our time, with nothing given, can we create an intellectual basis for belief in a free society? Or can we only prove the existence of individual freedom independent of and divorced from society? Since the rise of classical liberalism such a possibility has not really been conjured with or seen as possible. The old question of the individual and society was never seen in these terms; the very point about the state of nature was that such a condition was in fact not freedom. It was assumed that once measures had been taken to secure the freedom of the individual, a free society would of necessity ensue; since it was impossible to see any distinction between social and individual freedom, free individuals would make social freedom. But today, while it is still impossible to see how a free society can exist without free individuals, perhaps free individuals can exist within an unfree society. It is possible to contemplate such a development because we have (1) an asocial or antisocial attitude resulting from the inability of our age to believe that our society gives form and structure to freedom; and (2) an age of abundance that has made it feasible for the first time for an individual—perhaps a goodly number of them—to hack out his own private area of independence, even in a system in which all the main forces are working against freedom—his as well as everyone else's.

Stated in this bald form, the situation sounds ghastly as well as impossible. But let no one be surprised, for it is precisely the kind of freedom that seems most feasible to many liberals today.

We have not thought of anything better or different to replace the particular combination of freedom and form that derives from classical liberalism, radical liberalism, and socialism, and which today is no longer of use. Not being able to devise a social form within which freedom can operate, individual liberty in an unfree society is the best we can manage. There have even been attempts to justify such a condition, to establish it on a reasoned basis, as Riesman's *The Lonely Crowd* and Whyte's *The Organization Man* testify. The popularity of such works indicates that they touch a sensitive spot. No one else has come closer to finding a tolerable solution, no one else has held out such possibilities of hope. Here lies the tragedy of freedom today, its desperate character.

There would seem to be a general area of agreement on one point, at least, among the social critics, and that is that we are living in a society today that is increasingly unfree. To revise

Dunning's resolution, freedom has decreased, is decreasing, and ought to be enlarged. This agreement on the growing power of antagonistic forces is one of the more impressive and significant aspects of the current discussion in America and Great Britain. Granted that we do not yet have an altogether unfree society, granted that there are some counterforces working in favor of freedom, it is nevertheless true that almost no one is optimistic about the strength of those counterforces. The most that can be hoped for is to preserve a little area for the individual where he can retire after having been beaten by the organization, exhausted by affluency, frustrated by the other-directed. Whether the unanimous opinion that America and Great Britain are actually moving faster and faster toward the condition of an unfree society is correct, is only partially to the point. Just as important is the fact that this opinion exists, that the best minds of our time can see no present for us other than that of constricted freedom.

Is the individual in his garden all that is left at the end of history as the story of liberty? It is quite possible, but some interesting questions must be raised: (1) How long can individual liberty be maintained against the forces at work in an unfree society? Can personal independence survive contamination? (2) Is the tremendous effort required of the individual in hacking away at the forces that threaten to pervert freedom in his personal realm so great that the hacking process may become an end in itself and thus a sort of perversity of refusal? How free can the man be whose time is perpetually occupied in saying No! to society? (3) How many individuals can achieve this boon for the self in a society in which the main forces tend to suppress freedom? A small minority? A large majority? A handful of the chosen? If only a minority, what becomes of fraternity and equality? Or were the French wrong when they postulated that all men were free or none were free? Is it really possible to hide away with one's hi-fi set and ignore the rest of mankind or at least the majority of mankind? (4) If it is possible to do so, then what happens to society in such a situation? Does it maintain itself simply on the technical level of electronics, sewers, and bombers while each man strives to return to his own private version of the state of nature? (5) Finally, and most important, if freedom must contain the elements of expansion of opportunity and the possibility of adventure, can it be said that a private area of liberty is freedom at all? Does it not rather become a defense mechanism, useful and indeed necessary, but only the infrastructure of an adventure that never happens?

Perhaps these questions should not be asked in a time when the assumption of a social order, good for man and society, is more difficult to make than it was in the old days of liberal faith. Perhaps we should say that some freedom is better than none, especially now when the words "free society" can raise our hackles because we have seen so many societies that have forced men to be "free." It is important to understand that one reason we have such difficulty in even thinking about a free society is we have learned the hard way that it may mask the most terrible coercion of all. Thus our dilemma is doubled; we not only find it difficult to conceive of a free society, we are afraid to think about it. We have had, not to put too fine a point on it, enough of "free societies."

Unfortunately, the need to think about the meaning of a free social order becomes the more imperative the closer we come to its opposite. What is an unfree society in the West today? It is clearly not totalitarian, nor is it a dictatorship. In what sense then, can we, with our constitutional liberties intact all around us and growing more secure every day, talk of an unfree society, a system in which freedom is harried and indeed threatened in its very existence?

We can talk of an unfree society today in the context of a

lower world of insurgent anarchy, which beats constantly but unsuccessfully on the barricaded doors of the upper world of bureaucratic, organized insolence. Indeed, this is probably the way most Americans and Britons see their society.

Insurgent, individualized, and privatized anarchy is hard to destroy—indeed, impossible to destroy, for it is eternal, truculent, and sullen, and is given to rude remarks about its governors. The ways in which it is expressed are varied, often weird, and almost always formless and fugitive. Its angry young desire is to be left alone, and in defense of that desire it often acquires a vicious delinquent edge. Found not just among the so-called working classes, the phenomenon manifests itself variously as beats, hipsters, sit-in-ers, or marchers.

Anarchy has limits in insurgency because it lacks form. The upper world of organized, bureaucratic power cannot quell the rebel but neither can the rebel unseat its governors. For the governors dispense not only insolence but the brutality that comes with it. They have even discovered techniques that make it possible for their insolence to be accepted with gratitude by The Many as material and worldly favors. However, this upper world has its limits, for it is not a permanent elite but simply those who happen to hold power at any given moment. The result is not only confusion about what to do with its power but internal division, internecine bickering, frustration, and futility. Such men will never really advance an attack on insurgent anarchy except when they spasmodically try to winkle it out of its hiding places. Hence the real possibility of a deadlock between the two worlds; and in the deadlock, the loss of society to both.

The Difficulty and Danger of Being a Social Critic

If the loss of society is the gulf between upper and lower worlds the social critic comes into being as a creature of this split. His role and function is to describe a society as it becomes obnoxious to those who live in it and to tell why it is obnoxious. His role is to criticize, to show what is wrong; but paradoxically, at the same time to show that society has ceased to be meaningful. His criticism is not ideological, postulating an aim and proposing concepts of society; nor is it that of a reformer who accepts his society in the large but not in detail. Rather the social critic is one who, not allowing his penetrating vision to be blurred by ideology, uses the most impeccable data harvested from a crest of IBM cards to prove that the life of everyman is a product of a chaotic social existence of which everyman is unhappily and unwittingly a part. Society becomes an engine devoted to his manipulation and captivity. The critic may or may not make an effort to indicate tentative paths out of the slough of despond, but his main purpose, his main impact, lies in his demonstration of the existence of the slough that is society. He is devoted to explaining the sense of futility that seems to possess the members of his society and which he believes can be traced to its structural characteristics. He looks through a glass darkly; he acts the wrathful prophet who has a vision of doom and does not hesitate to tell his listeners about it.

The name "social critic" is not, therefore, an accurate description of his role. He is in fact an *asocial* critic because he himself embodies the very sense of loss of society that he finds to be the distressing symptom of his own era. He usually has—not always, it should be pointed out—an acute sense of the need for social order, and he is pained to find his own society such a gimcrack affair. He knows the cost of bearing the burden of the loss of society; he knows that the simple-minded and abstract "freedom-from" that conservatives prattle about is the loss of society itself, is a return to a state of nature. But it is precisely his knowledge of the fundamental importance of society, of the people around one, of The Other, that creates the dilemma for him and turns him into something that can be called an asocial critic. Finding that his society cannot support the needs that human beings have and the freedom of which he can conceive, and lacking the sense of history that will enable him to discover a drive to a new and different and better state of affairs, he must of necessity either turn away from the society in which he lives or create a utopia. Can he act as a social critic without at the same time forcing himself and his readers into a position of withdrawal from the very thing he is trying to achieve—freedom within and through society?

It is necessary to sympathize with him in this dilemma. It is not easy to maintain the balance between criticism and belief, to attack present-day society without becoming in the act antisocial or asocial. Particularly it is not easy without an ideological framework to establish the necessary relationships between society and freedom, a framework most social critics have either forsworn or which is too decrepit for use in this particular era. But the social critic is greatly impressed with the hell that society has become—a padded and rather comfortable hell, to be sure. And, as everyone knows, the best thing to do about hell is to get out of it.

Thus today the temptation to escape from society to freedom. We are surrounded with mass societies, with totalitarian systems, with all-encompassing techniques of social control that are enough to frighten anyone. The stimulating sense of tension that once could be thought to exist between the individual and society, a nourishing and necessary tension, has turned into a brutal and distinctly unhealthy and exhausting relationship in which the tensions run all one way and that destroys rather than fructifies. Once again, the liberal faces his problem with nothing given. Neither the good old liberal assumptions about man and society, nor the comfortable hopes of the radical-community mongers, are good or comfortable today. How, then, shall liberal man face the problem? How can he redefine the connection between freedom and society? Is there a connection? Or has freedom simply become flight from society?

Individual Freedom as Ca' Canny

One way to answer such questions is to accept the existence of the gap between society and the individual and make the most of it, indeed to use this gap to further the supposed independence of the individual. David Riesman has gone further in this direction than any other social critic and has produced the most effective description of how the individual can find his freedom by himself.

Cataloguing and pegging individuals and their writings is an odious and misleading activity, but it is clear that the ideas of David Riesman as expressed in *The Lonely Crowd* fall under the rubric of orthodox liberal. The phrase "orthodox liberal" is meant to indicate simply the general congruence of Riesman's thought with twentieth-century American liberal thought. Disenchanted though he may be, and no one can doubt that he is, he still remains within the spectrum of pragmatic, instrumental, Deweyite, reformist, democratic liberal ideas. But what is as significant as his congruence with that thought is his disenchantment not with its values but with the possibility of realizing them in today's society.

Riesman has a keen sense of the perils of freedom today as they impinge directly on the individual. He retains most of the classical liberal preoccupation with the position of the individual face to face with society and with the struggle that must ensue between the two. But in no sense does his thought represent a return to classical liberalism or an attempt to revive it. Rather it is an effort to find out in concrete and specific form and in individual and hence realistic terms exactly what kind of freedom is possible in our present social system. When Riesman talks about "individualism reconsidered" he means what he says.

The classical liberal of the nineteenth century saw the relationship between society and the individual not only in terms of struggle but in terms of a fructifying struggle, for it was out of this engagement that freedom arose. What is most noteworthy, on the other hand, about Riesman is his sense of the uselessness of struggle between the individual and society; therefore whatever conflict exists is killing, not fructifying, and certainly not conducive to freedom or anything except acute and stultifying anxieties. In so viewing the crisis of the individual he passes not only far beyond the bourn of the classical liberal but also beyond the limits of twentieth-century liberal thought, of which he is in part representative. He carries that thought into new realms where the individual is found not in a perpetual yet enthusiastic struggle with society, but simply with his back against the wall.

Being a realist, Riesman takes today's gap between the individual and society as the starting point in his particular search for freedom. How can man be free today in the face of a world composed of the other-directed? His answer is that the individual can only find freedom by withdrawal into personal autonomy. Freedom is not something to be discovered and used through activity in society and does not exist as a result of social order. Instead it must be wrenched away from society by the individual and transformed into personal autonomy. Prosperity may create a certain degree of independence for the individual, but such freedom will be effective only if it is used apart from society, by the individual in seclusion. Riesman, like Voltaire, failing to find a Garden of Eden, puts us into a Candidean garden.

This concept of freedom as ca' canny is freedom on the defensive against a society that is fundamentally and existentially—societies can have their existential role, too—structured against the individual. He operates on the same principle as the workman who stalls on the job within the exact routine established by the factory. He says, "I'll do my job, play my role, but that's all they're going to get out of me." Thus he protects his personal freedom from that society represented by the factory. Society in which freedom can have a venue and room for experiment and choice, ceases to exist and instead comes to be divided into the upper and lower worlds. Two of Riesman's concepts describe this cleavage: one is the powerless minority, the other the work-play antithesis.

The minority in question is that small group of personally autonomous that possesses what Riesman calls the "nerve of failure" and which is powerless precisely because it cannot cope with the other-directed society of which it is perforce a part. The "nerve of failure" is the possession of a defense against a superior power, and the ability to bear failure alone in contrast with a position that makes it possible to bear failure only as part of a crowd or group. By it the intellectual is protected from submitting to others because of his guilt feelings. It is needed to face the fact that a problem is unsolved and may be unsolvable; it also and as a corollary may make it possible to envisage practical possibilities.[2]

The failure of the autonomous man does not necessarily take place in the private sphere of his existence but in the workaday world in which there is no place by definition (i.e., Riesman's definition) for autonomy. It is this public world,

---

[2] David Riesman, *Individualism Reconsidered* (New York: The Free Press of Glencoe, 1954), pp. 39-54, 56, 69.

which we all see, hear, feel, and smell, and which engrosses most of our waking hours, that creates the failures of autonomous man. Left alone he presumably knows what to do with his freedom, but as a part of the social order he has little hope of doing anything with it. This society runs him even though it does not run itself very efficiently because of its other-directed qualities. Beneath the workaday world or outside it there lie areas of freedom that exist precisely because they have little or nothing to do with that world. In this arena freedom becomes, Riesman says,[3] a kind of looseness. But, a looseness from what? From the straitjacket of work, a straitjacket created and designed by the organization man and the other-directed.

The work-play antithesis has been heavily criticized, and Riesman himself has accepted much of the criticism in his new preface to *The Lonely Crowd*. As a description of the logic of the kind of society he describes and, it must be said, of the reality of much of American society today, it has the ring of accuracy. For by definition work has become meaningless in a highly organized society; therefore play is the realm in which the individual can find meaning through self-expression. "The productive impulse would have to be expressed in leisure and play." Work is bound to be unfree when it is something one does to satisfy a characterological urge to shine before one's fellows, or to fit in with one's fellows. (The other-directed, of course, seldom wish to shine; their main object is to acquire the dull finish that will enable them to fit in.) Work ceases to be invention; it becomes something done on cue and hence cannot be experienced as freedom. It is possible to envisage work as meaningful in an abstract sense, and Riesman can so envisage it; he also points out that expedients to erase guilt about work may not succeed because the source of

[3] *Ibid.*, pp. 163-164.

the anxieties may lie not in the meaninglessness of the work itself but in the guilt the other-directed feels about not being himself.[4] But whatever the case, work will never be a source of freedom to the other-directed, because he has no interest in objective skills.[5]

In Riesman's scheme of things the collapse of meaning in work and the feeling of powerlessness are in part the result of a lack of genuine commitment. Instead of a sense of passion about their work and a resulting conviction that life holds something worthwhile, men simply cling to existence without much enjoyment.[6] All that part of society that is subsumed under the category of work—and it is a great deal—becomes a place of nonfreedom. Work has lost its significance not because of its intrinsic qualities, but because the other-directed man refuses to choose the opportunities offered to him today by abundance. Instead he performs in the same way as the inner-directed did in the nineteenth century when work was necessary because of scarcity and when work could not be chosen or structured by choice. He does not, Riesman tells us, have to accept the older definitions of work. But because he is other-directed and not autonomous he does so and hence fails to achieve the "human need for active participation in a creative task."

Riesman's de-emphasis of work is one of the most important indications of his feeling of hopelessness and helplessness about the society of today as a place where freedom can be used. For work in and of itself cannot lose significance. The activity and actions are the same no matter where, when, or why they are performed. But the where, when, and why can vary considerably and in doing so can change the whole significance and role of work. What has changed, in Riesman's

[4] Riesman, *The Lonely Crowd*, p. 325.
[5] *Ibid.*, p. 135.
[6] Riesman, *Individualism Reconsidered*, p. 110.

view, is clearly the nature of society; in saying that work lacks significance he is saying that society lacks significance.

He drives this point home with the concept of play, which he posits against work, of play as a private concern. (Mainly as private, at least. Riesman does indicate that play can produce societies,[7] and hence has a social function, but he never follows up his hint. And it is clear that he regards play mainly as therapy in the present situation.) He says that "we should consider the possibility that, if the other-directed is to be made free, it will not be by work but by play."[8] But this play is, or should be, mainly an underground activity. It cannot be allowed to come into the public realm, to be a part of a social activity, because society by its very nature would kill it and make it not into the expression of spontaneity and freedom but into another dreary round of other-directed activity. He is, of course, careful not to deny the value of sociability; the autonomous man needs friends. But even here sociability is a personal choice that bears little or no relationship to society. There is sociability in Riesman's world but there is no fraternity.

Thus he postulates an escape to freedom from society, an escape made necessary by the fact that work has been degraded and that underground play alone remains as an outlet for free man. As a description of contemporary America one can hardly doubt its accuracy. Other social critics have come to virtually the same conclusion, although with less sense of the role of play in freedom. Both Paul Goodman and Hannah Arendt (in *The Human Condition*) not to mention William H. Whyte, Jr. (in *The Organization Man*), see modern society as one in which work has become problematical rather than fruitful. Attitudes toward work have clearly become a touch-

---

[7] Riesman, *The Lonely Crowd,* p. 325.
[8] *Ibid.*

stone of attitudes toward society because the two are so intimately bound together. Work as a means of expressing individual freedom in society is seen as only theoretically possible; in its place is the concept of work as an experience of nonfreedom. The resultant loss includes both work and society. Creativity and the freedom that goes with it are now conceived in terms of noncommunal play rather than working for or indeed even against society. As Riesman says, we should consider the possibility that, if the other-directed is to be made free, it will be not by work but by play. For whatever the theoretical possibilities in the work situation today, the other-directed because of his nature will reject them; he will continue to pretend that his work is important but in fact will fail to use it to experience autonomy. There, suddenly, autonomy will be snatched from him—by his own hand.[9]

[9] This attitude toward work results in a new liberal view about community. Work must be communal in today's or any society. It involves making commitments and decisions with others, and apart from a few of the intellectual trades—and even those are disappearing today as solitary activities—must of necessity involve group activities. Once the liberal desired nothing more than group activities and the community it implies. But today, with a few exceptions such as Erich Fromm's concept of the utopian community, the liberal looks upon the idea of community with real and deeply felt horror. For community today read the organization man and his social ethic. Community! Community now means only the modern misery of office work and bureaucratized corporations. Community is another word for exploitation, a word for what our society does to people. No doubt the ideal of community lingers on among liberals like an old refrain, but it is not for this world. In this world it is necessary to fend it off in order to protect whatever degree of personal autonomy can be won.

4

Images of Our Society

Do not civil politics presuppose something prior to or beyond the plain capacity for prudent compromise among the representatives of divergent views about how scarce income, opportunities, and honors should be distributed? Is not some attachment to the society as a whole, or to symbols of the society, something like a sense of the transcendent oneness of the civil society required for the system of civil politics to work?

EDWARD SHILS*

Riesman's thought embodies the loss of society in its most sophisticated form; the ideas of other social critics represent an attack on society that is focused not on the psychological damage society does but on its tendency to destroy itself as a meaningful experience.

Individual and society in the images of these critics now glower at each other across a profound gap. On one side is individual freedom turned ca' canny. On the other is society turned into a goods-producing machine that negates the very idea of social organization for mutual aid, comfort, and collective responsibility—as a place where men live together and share significant aspects of their existence.

The Organization Man Grows Up Absurd in an Affluent Society

Social criticism is a normal phenomenon of any society and can be expected to flourish no matter what the circumstances;

* Edward Shils, *The Guardian*, July 13, 1962.

if a country is poor it will be criticized because it is stunting the lives of its citizens and if it is rich because it is corroding their lives. Social criticism can lead to involvement in the affairs of society; it can show how the citizen is being mistreated or rejected and why he should be brought into the community. It can be concerned to bring about a proper relationship between society and citizen and to inform the individual that he is in fact a citizen even though society may have reneged on its responsibility to him. But it will do none of these if its image of society is only that of a machine to produce goods and if it presents the idea that the only possibility of salvation is through flight. Such is the situation of American social criticism today. It has become so obsessed with the idea that society is a supermarket on a superorganized scale that all it can envisage is the individual helpless in the face of this monolith. In the writings of our critics, present-day society is so totally condemned that—whether they mean it or not—the very idea of society itself is condemned. Given no alternative, what can they and their readers do but turn away from the whole idea of fraternity as an idea of brotherhood among men and of responsibility between one man and another? Given their concept of society as an affluent absurdity, how can they see social security as mutual help rather than a stack of IBM cards?

William Whyte's organization man is the most sweeping image of the hopelessness of our situation. For him the very phrase "social ethic" has become a means of reproach and danger. Looking upon society exclusively in terms of organization qua organization, he attacks bureaucracy as its most significant feature. He would have us fight bureaucracy, an excellent idea, which is negated, however, by his refusal to tell us what the conflict should be and could be about or to show that it might lead to a different society. The individual is to assert himself against the corporation; in doing so he will rid himself of the idea that the group is superior to the individual. But such attitudes are hortatory, not reflections on the social form—the group, if you will—within which freedom becomes a significant and lived reality, and they end in the bathos of how to cheat the corporation on its personality test.

They end, in other words, in the formless anarchy possessed by those who have escaped from society into the lower world of withdrawal—a sort of bargain beatnikism. One must add, of course, that fighting the corporation is an excellent thing and should be encouraged in every way. Yet it is also fruitless —the corporation, after all, is an immortal being, according to law and in fact—and ultimately the fight becomes somewhat tiresome. If that is what freedom is, it is not much. But face to face with the image of society-as-organization—and that is all it is to Whyte—the escape to a formless anarchy is feasible, attractive, and necessary. Politics—which is hardly mentioned by Whyte and is certainly not seen as an area of free and significant choice—and economics and everything else, including home life, are subordinated to this image of a glowering, devouring, gluttonous corporation. There is the upper world and the potentially lower world and there is nothing, no haven of pluralistic phenomena, in between. Whyte's contribution to social criticism is convincing evidence of how an image of what society is can establish an idea of what freedom must be. He also demonstrates how the loss of society reduces freedom to a pitiful thing.

Others, too, have this same sense of separation of the individual from society. Heilbroner, for example, tells us that the consequences of economic growth and its technological accompaniments are the weakening of the private person in his ability to cope with his social environment. Heilbroner points to the paradox of social life today: man is more a part of society, more involved in its doings, than ever before; but instead of being composed of those who are involved in a joint effort to realize the virtues of social existence, it is an "impersonal articulation of strangers into a working whole."[1]

Galbraith, although more cheerful in tone and more sprightly in suggesting solutions, also shows the same division of society into private and public realms; his *The Affluent Society* is an economist's and liberal's pained appreciation of the loss of society that occurs when private indulgence takes precedence over social existence. Galbraith, however, presents us with the other face of the coin. Where Riesman, Whyte, Heilbroner, and others show how society engulfs the individual and destroys his freedom, Galbraith describes the efforts of the individual to ignore the public good and to find satisfaction outside of society in his private garden—or, going Voltaire one better, in his own private swimming pool. Today people no longer even swim in common—among other things they do not do in common—because they lack a concept of a society which is anything other than a mechanical means for producing goods and affluence for private consumption. Since they lack any other idea of what society is or might be, naturally they flee it; why not? The net result is to compound the division of the social order into two halves, to make it more destructive of freedom rather than less.[2]

[1] Robert L. Heilbroner, *The Future as History* (New York: Harper & Row, 1959), pp. 73-74.

[2] Although today the conservative and liberal alike move away as rapidly as possible from society, the latter does so in a different spirit and for a different reason; his aim is to establish the grounds for personal autonomy, a basis on which to fight the corporation, to achieve a significant freedom rather than the ersatz freedom of having one's own swimming pool. He also recognizes what he loses when he flees society. Yet the liberal no less than the conservative feels that he must shake himself free of society if he is to survive. Thus for both, society clearly loses all significance and becomes merely a means of mechanical articulation, a sort of supercomputer; it obviously can no longer be a place in which freedom can be found or through which the sense of freedom can be experienced.

Galbraith's scheme of an upper world of organization producing useless goods and a lower world of individuals buying the useless goods, both in a high degree of affluence, comes about because of the lack of what he calls a social balance. It is from the lack of a balance between private and social goods that the loss of society emerges. This emphasis on quality—an emphasis completely and necessarily missed by a bourgeois, mechanistic, and goods-producing view of what social organization is for—is also fundamental to Paul Goodman's indictment.

When Goodman calls the society of today "absurd" he is not, like sicknik comedians,[3] doing so to make money but to make the most far-reaching attack on our system of any of the social critics. *Growing Up Absurd: Problems of Youth in the Organized System* starts off from the Riesman-Whyte approach but goes further and deeper into the problem of What's Wrong. Goodman is an old-fashioned radical; i.e., he believes in man's potential for goodness, rationality, and freedom and in the virtues and possibilities of fraternity in a way that is most unfashionable today. But the bite of his work comes not from the specific ideological content of this radicalism or even from his touch of controlled utopianism but from his fundamental radical impulse to reveal the roots of our society. Less interested than Riesman in theory, less personally involved than Whyte, Goodman is striving to grasp the particular quality of existence that modern society creates for those who live in it. That quality is its absurdity.

To call American society absurd is an interesting accusation, for if any society ever demonstrated a certain rigorous logic it would seem to be ours. The idea of the absurd as a popular philosophical and social concept grew up in Europe

[3] See Benjamin DeMott, "The New Irony: Sickniks and Others," *The American Scholar*, Winter, 1961–1962.

and gained its potency from the experience of revolution and
disorder in the twentieth century. America has been spared
such terrors. Instead it has pursued its course doggedly according to the canons of capitalism and it has succeeded. America
absurd? Surely not, given a few common-sense assumptions
and principles about economics and politics. But alas, if the
twentieth century has taught us nothing else, even in America,
it has taught us that common sense is often the most absurd of
all when the consequences of fine principles and solid assumptions are so far out of relationship to their aims that the dis-
junction between principle and consequence is all that can be
seen.

Such is the ironical meaning of Goodman's *Growing Up
Absurd* where the central absurdity appears in the achievements of a society so beautifully organized and articulated
that it has no worthwhile work for large and increasing num-
bers of its people! We have seen the decline of work as a central value in the writings of Riesman. Goodman brings the
dilemma into the open and in doing so indicates another form
of the loss of society. It has ceased to be a place of significant
human effort where men test themselves in common with
other men for common goals, where men can see the results of
their work in the creation of an impressive and even majestic
society, where they become aware of work as a social experience that is significant. Instead, it has become a gigantic and
frantic discount house in which labor input stands as counters
for so much goods of such-and-such quality. Instead of the
Good Society we now have the Goods Society.

Goodman's criticism also reveals in a way no other social
critic does that the cost of fleeing society to find freedom in
the anarchic lower world is not light. Freedom below turns
out to be nothing else but that ugly thing, juvenile delin-
quency; as Alfred Kazin says in his discussion of Goodman,

"the 'absurdity' that many older people feel is the same one that many embittered, lost, and mutinous young people act on in incidents that get them into trouble, which indeed they often act on *in order* to get into trouble."[4] There is personal freedom below and outside the colossus above, but it takes on a different face in Goodman's consideration of it than it does in the description of it as "personal autonomy" or "fighting the corporation." (Hipsterism is, of course, the violent philosophy of such behavior, while beatnikism is its pacifist philosophy.) It ceases to have a tea-and-crumpets approach and becomes a matter of brutishness. And Goodman's point is that such "freedom" is what is to be expected if there is no society to make work worthwhile.

Thus he describes our society as "an apparently closed room." It is a system that he sees as fixed, that has no sense of history, and in which a wide variety of human characters run the show without believing in it. There are only the values of the rat race, which are held in contempt by everyone, and the general assumption that any new system would be like the first.[5]

Goodman is less scientific and more impressionistic than Riesman, less concerned with a theory of The Thing, but in their description of the quality of our society the two men are hardly at variance. Where he does depart from the Riesman approach is in his less optimistic view of the possibilities of finding a significant freedom through personal autonomy or any kind of autonomy in such a system. It is hard for Goodman to conceive of freedom apart from a significant and meaningful society. Certainly he recognizes the fact that it is possible to contract out of the system. But he also sees the

---

[4] Alfred Kazin, "Youth Is a Pressure Group," *The Reporter*, December 22, 1960.

[5] Goodman, *Growing Up Absurd* (New York: Random House, Inc., 1960), chap. 8.

futility and danger of this. The beats, despite his sympathy for them, are portrayed as a form of withdrawal from civilization; the parochial culture of the beats shows, in fact, how hard it is to produce value in the system of the closed room. To Goodman the word "beat" is all too accurate, for they are literally the defeated.

Yet, the most symptomatic aspect of his attitudes is the necessity he feels to give his loyalty to attempts to flee the closed room despite his recognition of the inherent loss involved in such attempts. In the end he cannot go much beyond Riesman's stand on personal autonomy as the only feasible solution to the problem of freedom in the face of the colossus that our society has become. Face to face with "It" he concludes that the best hope today lies in those who face existence with direct action, with the youth movements, which range all the way from action painting to the English Angry Young Men to those who participate in direct action in race relations. Goodman praises these people because they have given up role-playing and are at work with existential reality, a form of living that is in the most specific contrast with the organized system, the rat race, the closed room.

One can understand his point. Even the beats with their curious passivity are at grips with reality instead of being involved in playing the game. But, as with Riesman, the irony of Goodman's conclusion is that it is his sense of the fundamental importance of society that makes necessary his salutation to the existentialist actionists and their desperate attempts to break loose from a society dominated by Bureaucratic Insolence. As he points out, today it is necessary to choose between working with the system or getting out of it; it is in the nature of our situation that it does not seem possible to work at changing the institutions that threaten us. But for those who choose to revolt there is no available world to

give form to freedom. Society, in his view, is not only a cause
of our troubles; it is also the only real solvent of those
troubles. Anyone who thinks differently is not, as Goodman
loves to say, serious. But society today, to use the title of his
last chapter, is a "missing community." Existentialism is all
very well, and, to paraphrase Sir William Harcourt, "we are
all existentialists now," but it will not fill the gap of the missing community. When Goodman tells us that our economic
system is not geared to the creation of important goals for
which the young can work and that therefore to a young man
society becomes a racket instead of something serious, he has
told us the crucial problem that haunts the new search for
freedom. If society is a racket, then those within it will boon-
doggle and freedom will become simple waste for the lack of
anything serious to do.

The Mass Society

Of all the images of our society the most prevalent and
striking is that of a mass society.[6] It is also the image that
most clearly reveals the sense of the split between the upper
world of bureaucratic power and the lower world of insurgent
anarchy. We need not concern ourselves here with the endless
and sometimes tiresome discussions of mass culture, mass
leisure, mass communications, and the processes of massification which are themselves so much a feature of our society.
But a recognition of the implications of the concept will lead
us to understand some of the reasons why it is less and less
possible for the liberal to think hopefully about society.

The phrase "mass society" is a contradiction of terms. The
very essence of a so-called mass society is the *separation* of

[6] For a summary of American thought on the nature of a mass society, see
Leon Bramson, *The Political Context of Sociology* (Princeton, N.J.: Princeton
University Press, 1961).

people, one from another. It is a society in which the separated
individual is exploited by an elite. C. Wright Mills's analysis
of the position of the modern power elite and of its relationship to a mass society is a significant means of understanding
one of the essential features of such a social system, the way in
which the separated individual is used for the purposes of a
small group that purports to run the system. A mass society
is not directionless; it has an object and the object is exploitation. The form of exploitation may change; it may become
the exploitation of consumer urges rather than labor power,
but the same process is involved. The mass society more than
any other is one that is broken into the two halves of an upper
world of the system and a lower world of the disorganized. To
be sure, the latter, due to defects in the process of exploitation, are not always under the thumb of the upper world; but
when they escape they are not capable of any kind of action
except anarchy. Hence whenever they can escape from the
system—and such escapes are not infrequent; the mass society
knows also of mental emigration—they are not, by the very
nature of the society in which they live, because of its structure of separation, capable of doing anything about it, of
taking social actions. Riesman's personal autonomy, Whyte's
fight against the corporation, Goodman's ultimate reliance on
beatniks, are all ways of achieving freedom through escape
into the lower world of a mass society. The model of a mass
society is the ultimate statement of the liberal[7] nightmare.

A consideration of mass society demonstrates another aspect
of the dilemma that lies at the heart of liberal thought. As we
have seen, the liberal, in the face of this monster, feels the

[7] Needless to say, not only liberals make such an analysis, a fact that has
led to some confusion. There are some who feel that the liberal in putting
forward such a model becomes an elitist, and antidemocratic. See Professor
Lewis Coser's discussion of such attitudes in "Comments on Bauer and Bauer,"
Journal of Social Issues, Vol. XVI, No. 3 (1960).

necessity to separate himself from it and to look for freedom in the realm of personal autonomy. Such a separation in the abstract can undoubtedly lead to some kind of freedom. But an individual who withdraws from society even for such an excellent motive acts precisely in the way that a mass society wishes him to act. He withdraws from his fellowman and hence becomes incapable of helping them or protecting them from exploitation because now he is separate from them. Both they and himself are thereby weakened in their resistance. Withdrawal in whatever form establishes the conditions in which mass manipulation becomes *more* rather than less possible, for it aids the destruction of those intermediary groups that are the best defense against a mass society.[8] It does more. It destroys the idea of a whole society, of a Great Society (to use Graham Wallas' term), the very idea of society itself.

Privatization is the name of this trap. Privatization is the driving back of the citizen—if citizen is still the proper word —to his private concerns, to his own affairs, which are, by their nature, petty and of no concern to anyone else. He is driven back to privacy not because he values privacy as the highest good but because in a mass society he finds that it is the only act left to him. Society offers him nothing on which he can exercise his choice except consumer goods for private consumption, the preference for one can of beer over another; choice is reduced to its minimum, to its absurdity.

It is with this fact of private choice that the mass society reaches its logical limit, for it can never be sure about what is being done in the dark television room at home. Maybe the fellow has turned off the television set and gone to sleep. A disquieting situation. Yet it is a situation the mass society cannot overcome since, not being totalitarian, it cannot reach

[8] See William Kornhauser, *The Politics of Mass Society* (New York: The Free Press of Glencoe, 1959).

beyond a certain limit. It achieves its goal of separating people, one from the other. But what happens then? It is never quite sure.

Thus there is a degree of freedom—of a certain type—to be found in a mass society. The last laugh is after all with the human being. He is a crafty animal and not easily gotten down. But the mass society is crafty too. It may not win, but it gets most of what it wants. It gets individuals who can be pushed around and whose area of choice is increasingly limited to deciding between one brand of goods and another.

The liberal in his search for freedom is far from being unaware of the threat of privatization; he has an acute sense of the meaning of society to freedom. David Riesman especially has tried to come to grips with the problem and would insist, correctly, that there is a vast and crucial difference between privatization and personal autonomy. He is, indeed, careful to define personal autonomy as the ability to choose whether to join groups, rather than as the simple withdrawal from groups, which would be characteristic of privatization. But granting the possible existence of such autonomy in the kind of society the social critic himself describes, more questions are raised than are answered.

It is now necessary to look at what the loss of society means for the present condition of liberal thought. What are the implications of the split between the upper and lower worlds for the liberal idea of freedom?

Boredom in the Marketplace

The sense of this split is derived not just from a fear of the conformity that the upper world imposes, but from a whole trend of Western society toward centralization, bureaucratization, and structural rigidity, which in themselves may be neither bad nor good but which nevertheless are seen by the social critic as productive of nothing but society as a market-place. The greatest irony presented by America in a time of unprecedented wealth, an affluence that the social critics themselves were the first to point out, lies in the volume of protest affluence has called into being. American society today has been called many things, most of them bad. But the one thing it has never been called is "the Successful Society." Yet successful is precisely what it is—in its own terms. Certainly no one, liberal or otherwise, can complain about affluence as such. But the quality of the social organization in which affluence is encased is a legitimate concern, a concern that is bottomed on the total nature of a society in which the problems of affluence are only a particular manifestation of a deeper reality and of the historical developments of the twentieth century.

It is this deeper reality, and not the specifics of American society, that is seen by the liberal as the threat to freedom today and that postulates a need for a new search for freedom. Although it is impossible to sum up the multifractured vision of the social critics in one word, if that word had to be chosen it could be said that they see today's society as meaningless. It is astounding that a society that is so neatly articulated on an economic and technical plane, so rational in its material endeavors, should be seen as meaningless and absurd. Meaningless in what sense? In the sense that the society is inherently, not accidentally, of no fundamental interest, of no concern, in relation to that quality that is the unique possession of the human being, his ability to be free through the exercise of significant choice. No doubt the society works well; no doubt the goods are produced and some of them are even useful. But the production of goods is not in and of itself an interesting process once whatever problems it poses have been resolved.

Thus the irony of affluence; the better-organized this society becomes, the less interesting, significant, and meaningful it becomes. Just to the extent that it solves its problems of goods production, to that extent it deserves only a colossal yawn. It simply does not matter whether the cost of the illth produced today decreases or whether its quality goes up. For no significant human choice is involved in choosing between one piece of illth and another. And hence to be drawn into this society, to take it seriously, to engage oneself in the selling of, say, a particular brand of cigarettes, is to lose at the very least a significant area of one's freedom by becoming a part of a meaningless system. There are certain fields of endeavor, of course, that are exciting and that engage man's freedom; science is preeminently such a field today. But the system as a whole bumps and grinds, thumps and clatters, and pours out its goods in more or less profusion, in better or worse quality, and they are dutifully consumed. But unless one takes those goods seriously—and that one cannot do—society itself cannot be taken seriously.

Thus it is not merely the disciplinary aspects of society that cause the social critics to turn away from it. It is not merely that it forces a person to be other-directed if he is to survive, but that the thing for which he submits to other-direction is not worth the sacrifice.

The significance of this concept of social meaninglessness for the liberal lies in its message that not only must he disengage himself from society to protect himself but that *he cannot engage himself* in this society, that there is no way in which he can employ his capacity to choose. Even his work, the prime and main form of his social activity, takes on the character of confronting indistinguishable and unimportant alternatives—if one can call such insipid encounters a confrontation.

When the liberal mounts this accusation he is drastically

modifying his traditional argument on the threats to and problems of freedom. It is a modification that underlies the whole liberal malaise and that undercuts his whole position.

Previously he saw society as a threat in the sense that it could and would take freedom away from the individual by preventing him from acting, by imposing restraint on his actions. Accordingly, there was a conflict between the individual and society that had to take place in society. Only by changing the system could those restraints be removed. Society, in this case, was not meaningless; it held a great deal of significant meaning if for no other reason than because it was the source both of despotism and of a future freedom. Thus private freedom depended upon public freedom and public activities. There was, as there has always been, a keen sense of the difference between private and public spheres but there also was, as there is not now, a keen sense that the two overlapped, that society was a place of useful struggle. There was a sense that what happened to society was important, was either a victory or a defeat for freedom.

But when society is seen as meaningless and because it is seen as meaningless, such struggles can no longer take place. There are no victories—or defeats—in a situation that does not allow any significant choice. Society is despotic again but with the difference that now the individual is free to do anything as long as it is not important. What baffles the liberal is that ours is the first non-totalitarian society that cancels the struggle to give freedom a form. It does this by not allowing any definition of new objectives; the process of other-direction and the imposition of a social ethic (to use Riesman's and Whyte's terms) aim exclusively and by definition at perpetuation of the existent situation. Basic issues are never raised because it is the very essence of this society not to raise them.

It is true, there are still areas of significant choice today.

Yet, even though cheerfulness insists on breaking in, the problem that the liberal has posed for himself is not one that can be avoided in reality or in theory. The whole defensive posture of the liberal today is explicable in terms of his fear and suspicion of the meaningless qualities of his society.[9] And the problems that his defensiveness has created can only be seen in the context of those fears and suspicions. Certainly one must ask whether this defensive posture has solved any of the problems that the liberal himself has posed for freedom. His tragedy is that he is more acutely aware of his own loss and what it signifies than anyone else.

[9] The lack of any concrete idea of what social freedom can be is not unrelated to the anti-ideological position taken by some (not all) liberals in recent years. Because the liberal has not been able to develop any ideas about society except that of retreat, it would seem that ideological differentiation is at an end, that we are now all of us members of a nation of like-minded consensus-seekers of one variety or another. Leaving aside the chicken-and-the-egg question of whether the retreat from society is a result or a cause of anti-ideological thought, the important question is what such retreat signifies. The clash between liberal thought and conservative thought remains despite the liberal retreat; he has no more in common with the conservative than he ever had. But if the liberal has not joined the conservative in an unholy consensus, without an ideology he has no social concepts to fit into his idea of freedom. The liberal today still has—and justly so—his sense that what he seeks is different from what the conservative seeks, for the latter does not seek freedom at all, but stasis. But what he lacks is the ideological content with which to embody in concrete fashion what he means by freedom.

The loss of society and the loss of ideology are tied together simply because the liberal has minimized the ideological content of his thought by his retreat from society. He has, of course, an ideology, but it is one less concerned with action in society and more concerned with action in the private sphere. In this situation the relevance of his ideology to social problems is limited and minimized. By ceasing to focus on the question of how to find freedom in society, his ideology ceases to be an ideology of public affairs (a fact that is revealed by the more popular manifestations of this trend). Thus on the public level the liberal, for all his magnificent descriptions of modern society, ceases to operate in terms of ideology while he continues to do so on the private level. This curious and unique shift of emphasis is the result of what might be called the unwriting of, or disillusionment with, the traditional liberal ideology of public affairs. While the conservative has been busily developing such an ideology, the liberal has been busily dismantling his. One is entitled, therefore, to ask of those liberals who prattle of the "end of ideology": What ideology has come to an end? Whose ideology has come to an end? The answer is: the public ideology of the liberal.

Cultural Pessimism and the Loss of Society

Such is the logic of the meaningless society that the liberal sees around himself and that has led him to postulate that freedom can exist only in a private sphere. It is a sociopolitical logic and vision that is closely related to the twentieth-century literary and philosophical vision of a meaningless civilization. Political and social thought in the hands of the social critics has taken on the form of a general cultural critique. A brief consideration of the coincidence between their attack on society and the more generalized despair of Western intellectuals of our time will show not only that it is a whole society that is under attack, but that manifestations of the loss of society are not confined to the social critics. Its roots lie deep in the cultural pessimism of our century, in the fear and distrust of society which has become a staple of Western intellectual thought.

One aspect of this thought has been well summarized by Ihab Hassan in his discussion of the contemporary American novel: "So long as it was possible to mediate between Self and World, the anarchy in the heroic soul remained covert; the hero appeared as a hero. But the World in our time seems to have either vanished or become a rigid and intractable mass. The anarchy of nihilism and the terror of statism delimit the extremes between which there seems to be no viable mean. Mediation between Self and World appears no longer possible—there is only surrender or recoil."[10]

The recoil of the contemporary American novelist in turn rests upon an earlier recoil of the intellectual after World War I when, as Irving Howe has pointed out, the American intellectual had to face the fact of a collapse of values and the consequent necessity of living in terms of personal assertion.

[10] Ihab Hassan, *Radical Innocence: Studies in the Contemporary American Novel* (Princeton, N.J.: Princeton University Press, 1961), p. 327.

What Howe calls a "search for a moral style" was born from revulsion against the moral disorder of the capitalistic society of the 1920's. It was a refusal of new values to put in place of the old and a rejection of idealism with its large-scale beliefs. Instead there was the attempt to live simply with "a fragmentary code of behavior by which to survive decently. . . ." Intellectuals were left with "the desire to salvage from the collapse of social life a version of stoicism that can make suffering bearable. . . ." It was the ruin of social life that drove such writers to such positions: "In almost all of Hemingway's books there is a tacit assumption that the deracination of our life is so extreme, everyone must find a psychic shelter of his own, a place in which to make a last stand."[11]

Alfred Kazin has also pointed out that the "apocalyptic wish" found in, for example, the beats, has its origins in "the stated enmity between the self and the world . . . a tension which was set up by romanticism and which Freudianism has sharpened and intensified. . . ." This enmity, this sense that the external world is "alien" will not find its resolution in Freudianism because it is ". . . a critique of Victorian culture; it is not a prescription for living in the twentieth century, in a world where the individual finds himself increasingly alienated from the society to which he is physically tied."[12] Thus Kazin postulates against an alien world the plea of Iris Murdoch that "we need to return from the self-centered concept to the other-centered concept of truth." The difference in the attitude with which Kazin and Murdoch approach The Other in comparison with Riesman, Whyte, *et al,* need not be underlined.

[11] Irving Howe, "In Search of a Moral Style," *New Republic,* September 25, 1961.
[12] Alfred Kazin, "The Language of Pundits," *Atlantic Monthly,* July, 1961. For an interesting discussion of some analogous ideas in Great Britain see Donald Davie ("Towards a New Aestheticism?") and Raymond Williams ("Literature and Society") in *The Guardian,* July 21 and August 11, 1961.

The loss of society in twentieth-century thought is firmly grounded on a characteristic cultural disenchantment. But it is also the result of the liberal disillusionment with the history of twentieth-century politics. Among the most discouraging aspects of that history as the liberal looks back from the present is the record of his own political movements, those movements that can be considered to be the embodiment, however imperfect, of his principles. He recognizes, of course, that the New Deal in America or the Labor Party in Great Britain, for example, are the very pillars of progress and freedom. Yet he also recognizes that their accomplishments have done little or nothing to forestall the coming of the type of society that is castigated today by the liberal-turned-social-critic. Hence he can hardly feel any confidence that politics can resolve the issues created by an affluently absurd society.

The doubts held by the liberal today concerning the efficacy of politics are not simply the expression of the liberal's eternal refusal of power. Rather they are doubts about the ability of politics today to transcend the society of which they are a part and to effect change, to create the conditions of freedom. A consideration of the framework of liberal thought with which the Kennedy administration began its operations will indicate the gap between the man in power, the official liberal who has succeeded to office, and the social critic who finds a whole society contaminated by a power elite, other-direction, or whatever may be his particular curse. Between these two there is little in common. The one, pressed by the necessities of making decisions in a complex political environment, is committed to the ethos of planning as a way of resolving particular policy issues. The other, free of facing the problem of actually getting things done, is committed to a rejection of the fundamental qualities of his society. The one is enmeshed in the politics of society, the other is divorced from the politics of society.

5

The Planned Society
of Official Liberalism

We must get America moving again.
—PRESIDENT JOHN F. KENNEDY

America has absorbed the liberalism of the New Deal years into its bones; although it has been witness to a conservative revival of no mean proportions—or perhaps one should say, of mean proportions—it has nevertheless elected a president who has surrounded himself with advisors whose approach to politics can be grouped under the rubric of liberalism. It is, of course, liberalism with a difference; chastened and hardened by disappointment, it has to live on the "nerve of failure" postulated by Riesman. Yet if it is chastened—if it is "post-liberal"[1]—it has also had such a wide measure of acceptance that it can be said to be an official ideology, an ideology appropriate to the officialdom of bureaucracy and politics, and appropriate, too, for the expert who works with and for government. It is official in the sense that it has become the typical, patterned way of thought of a liberal "establishment," using the word establishment in the British sense of a group with a secure place in the universe of power,

[1] See Eric Goldman, "The 'New' First Hundred Days," *University: A Princeton Magazine*, Spring, 1961.

society, and thought. It has, indeed, become so official, so established, and such a routine way of thinking, that today a conservatism that wishes to go back so that we may stand still can actually seem radical to many persons.

As the legatee of the New Deal, official liberalism today is as busy and as useful as the older liberalism ever was in manipulating a whole society; indeed, in many areas it has a firmer and more thoughtfully inclusive grip on the concrete realities and needs of American society. But does it have anything to say to those who are concerned with the problems defined and images created by the social critics, who see society as split into two halves, with the resulting loss of society? Does official liberalism show any sign of offering the critics and their followers a political movement that meets their needs and that can therefore act as a means of giving them a political focus? Or will it conduct itself in such a way that the rupture between the upper and lower worlds will be paralleled by the split between official liberalism and social criticism?

The answer lies in the future, since the record of the Kennedy administration will not be written until it has run its terms. Further, it must be said that it is easier to ask questions than it is to cope with the environment in which the hard policy decisions must be made. Let us at least honor an administration of which it is possible to ask such questions. Also, more significant change may emerge by 1969 from the piling up of piecemeal actions than meets the eye in 1964. Yet the problem remains. Is there any reason to believe that official liberalism will so modify the power realities of America that freedom can be something other than a flight from society?

To consider that question it will be necessary to ask first what the phrase "official liberalism" means—it should not be identified only with the Kennedy administration since it could also be found among certain segments of the Eisenhower administration—and what it has in mind for American society, what plans have been maturing behind the worried brows of the experts who have seen America become increasingly a planner's nightmare.

Two works, whose purpose was to scrutinize America and to decide on its goals, give an indication of the content of official liberalism. As a representative selection of the writings of the intellectual elite who are mainly committed to its canons, these essays enable us to understand its intellectual qualities on the eve of the Kennedy administration. Such a description of plans and hopes and aims is not, of course, a description of that administration. It does, however, reveal the concrete attitudes toward American problems that were held by the official liberal and indicates what he would do if he had the power.

One of those works was produced by the outgoing administration—a fine time, one might think, for an administration to think about goals, but typical of the Eisenhower administration. It was written by the President's Commission on National Goals and was called *Goals for Americans*. The other, produced for the incoming administration, was composed of "task force" reports prepared under the title *New Frontiers for the Kennedy Administration*. In preparing *Goals for Americans* over one hundred experts were used as consultants; fourteen experts were asked to write essays for the Commission—which evidently could not write its own essays—and the Commission itself numbered eleven. There was a staff of five and the job was administered by the American Assembly of Columbia University. Taken as a whole it was a Big Operation, and one may assume that it was intended to produce something rather definitive. The Kennedy reports, on the other hand, have the flurried appearance which that administration has adopted from its master. Some, as published, are sketchy to the point of uselessness, others are of some limited importance, and one is a minor masterpiece—Dean Landis' report on the administrative agencies. As revelations of the nature of official liberalism today, and taken together, they offer a useful insight into the mind of the planner at work.

The official liberal approach to the problems of our society can be described as a point of view that looks to planning as the solvent of our discontents without any fundamental concern for the political or ideological source of those discontents. Planning in the hands of the official liberal would provide the solutions to the specific malfunctioning from which America suffers today; once our diseases are identified the planner can get to work and eradicate them through human action and intelligence. Man should use whatever means are at hand to solve his problems—the idea of problem-solving is basic to this neo-New Dealism—and in practice the means at hand usually end up as the federal government. It also ends up in the hands of the expert who accepts the existing framework of pluralism and ignores all those doubts about democracy, equality, reason, science, pragmatism, and mass persuasion that today have bedeviled so many intellectuals and the social critics in particular. For if the expert did not ignore such questions there would be little basis for his survival as an expert. It is on such unexamined concepts that he literally depends for his professional life. And it is necessary to understand that such dependence is not a question of financial self-interest but of his fundamental project as an expert—to *do*.

The hopes and assumptions of the experts revolve around various areas of American life that present unresolved questions and that seem to the official liberal to demand concrete, practical answers. Is the problem one of urban disorganization? Catherine Bauer Wurster's excellent study on a "Framework for an Urban Society" in *Goals for Americans* proposes to seize upon the crisis of urban disorganization in order to plan the kind of urban area in which we wish to live. She is the most radical of the experts, for she points out that it will be necessary to make some basic decisions about the way we really want to live and that it will be necessary to use big government and not the broken-down local government units we now have if we are to rebuild our cities. Is the problem education? Then John Gardner (president of Carnegie Corporation) believes we should innovate in education, and that innovation will not come about unless governments on all levels plan what to do. Is the problem one of economics? Professor Samuelson for President Kennedy and two experts from the Committee for Economic Development for the Goals Commission are in fundamental agreement that government planning for growth is both necessary and feasible; indeed, economics in their hands becomes a technical matter. Culture, too, will come under the aegis of planning, for August Hecksher in *Goals for Americans* would have the government create a home for art and would have both private and public funds used to establish repertory theaters.

In the Kennedy task force reports, area redevelopment, social welfare, education, and cultural affairs are all conceived as involving not just government but government planning on a continuing basis. The Landis report on administrative agencies, the only one really to rise above minutiae, is concerned not only to clean up the agencies in the sense of de-corrupting them and making it possible for them to get through their work, but also to make them into effective policy-planning instruments. He would do more, for not only would he have the agencies take on responsibilities for planning, but various agencies would be grouped into integrated wholes to meet the demands of more general planning than any one agency can cope with. He mentions transportation, communications, and energy as areas in which coordination is essential. We are not ready yet, he thinks, for a ministry of transportation with cabinet rank, but that should not and need not prevent the evolution of a "national transportation policy." And, of course, his famous recommendation on strengthening the chairman of the agencies is part of his hope for making them effective policy-making bodies instead of Dickensian circumlocution offices.

The New Deal has returned. It is, however, a tamed and housebroken New Deal; no official liberal now speaks about "economic royalists," though we have, in fact, more economic royalists than ever before. Housebroken, the official liberal is ready to enter into the drawing rooms of the Mighty. What kind of society will it create for us and how adequate will it be in facing the real problem of today?

Above all else, a society under the stimulus of official liberalism will be a "clean, well-lighted place."[2] It will be as neat and orderly as American life will allow. It will be the welfare state plus. Plus what? Plus all the awful joys of American free-enterprise capitalism, which, however, will be allowed to go so far and no further. Education will be widespread and get better in quality. The executive branch of government will become a super-planning agency, having to do battle with Congress, no doubt, but still getting its way on all the big decisions. The mass entertainment industry will continue to ruin our dispositions, but there will be increasing opportunities for what are euphemistically called "minority interests." Health, it need hardly be said, will be as perfect as our climate permits. Farm surpluses will pile up but better uses will be made of them and eventually—sometime in the next century

[2] With apologies to Kathleen Nott, who has recently used that phrase as the title of a book on Sweden.

—they may even begin to shrink slightly through strict government control over the half-dozen farmers who will remain to feed the rest of us. They will also shrink because we will be eating more; the "report" of the Goals Commission contains this odd sentence: "Improvement of nutritional levels for many Americans would not only increase the work efficiency of our population but also reduce the farm surpluses." Finally, the economy, needless to say, will provide abundant leisure and affluence for the most wayward of individuals. No one, except perhaps some millions of Negroes, Puerto Ricans, and other miscellaneous types, will be allowed to escape affluence. And with all this we will still be able to look back and say that these things were set forth in the Declaration of Independence.

Such extrapolations, though accurate in fact, are unfair in tone, for it must be remembered that a clean, well-lighted place is far better than a dirty, ugly, and violent place. Faced as we are with the possibility of what might be called a partial utopia or pseudo-utopia under the direction of the planners of official liberalism, it must be stressed that this is no time for the easy romanticism that says that planning crushes the human spirit, etc. It does nothing of the kind; it can help liberate the human spirit; and the society described above is far better than that we have now, by any liberal criteria. The only people who would not find it better are the conservatives —for the Declaration of Independence notwithstanding, the conservative ethos is going to take some hard knocks in such a society—or those eccentric radicals who would join hands with the conservatives in praise of dirt and individualism. Indeed, just to get our cities painted and the streets washed would be a major achievement. No, romanticism will not help us now. The partial utopia of the official liberal may have some amusing features, but they will be more tolerable than the not-very-amusing aspects of our present society.

One of the virtues of official liberalism can be seen in the emphasis it places on science not as an operational technique to achieve "better things for better living" but for its intellectual content. Both the essay by Warren Weaver on science in *Goals for Americans* and the task force report (Jerome Wiesner, chairman) on space investigation in *New Frontiers of the Kennedy Administration* stress science as a value in itself. The degradation of science into a means to a better gadget or to prove the superiority of our leadership over that of the Russians is one of the great weaknesses of present society; some official liberals at least see that the importance of science is to be found in the excitement of investigation. Mr. Weaver's essay especially stresses the importance of investigation as such and also points out that for all the money the United States is supposed to spend for science it actually spends very little.

If the values of official liberalism—within their limits—are sound, they nevertheless contain some important lacunae. For one cannot help wonder how different a clean, well-lighted place would be in terms of power, or more precisely, in terms of democracy, than our present dirty, slovenly, and exploitative place. It is, after all, possible to consider that bourgeois democracy has certain virtues without succumbing to its fundamental assumptions concerning class and power.

Who would really run this new society? Granted that things —literally, things—would be better and better organized under the official liberals, would the same power structure, the same class structure, that we now possess remain in the new world? It is better to be pushed around in a clean city than a dirty city, but one is still being pushed around. In one sense, these problems are raised by Mills's *The Power Elite*, and whatever the virtues and faults of his particular analysis it is nevertheless true that the question we face is how the present structure of power can preferably be destroyed and if not destroyed then at least modified. It is the recognition that this is our problem today which has already given the New Deal a dusty place on the history shelves. No doubt the New Deal helped us to get to a cleaner and better-lighted place than we were in during the 1930's. But its refusal to tamper with the basic facts of power helped to confirm its past and present distribution, and raises questions as to how meaningful democracy can be in clean, well-lighted places.

Thus it is necessary to ask whether the commitment of the official liberal to planning necessarily assumes, in the America of today and the future, not a technocracy or even a managerial elite—bad enough though they are—but the present bourgeois society with its exploitation, or whether it will lead to fundamental changes in the nature of our society. One of the gravest weaknesses of official liberalism, for all its considerable virtues, is its failure to face the question posed by planning; does the planning in question affect in any significant way the power of some men over other men? It may well be that it does; there are certain important possibilities in planning as far as equality is concerned. But the case is seldom examined by the official liberal. And since it is not, his planned society in and of itself and without some kind of value-ideological concept in support of it is not likely to bring the fundamental changes that are necessary. Hence, too, the peculiar fact that his planning, instead of having that dynamic quality usually ascribed to it, is static in its approach to the basic realities of society.

All of which is to mount the accusation against official liberalism that its commitment to democracy, which is indeed fundamental to its being, is nevertheless more abstract than real. Democratic beliefs today are widespread and the official liberal is their prime carrier. But democratic concepts are in disarray, they are more disheveled, more disorganized than they have ever been. In this case we are far removed indeed from the neatness and organization of a clean, well-lighted society. The very virtue of official liberalism—its ability to cut through the waverings of intellectual self-doubt—plays it false when it is faced with the problem of democracy. For the question of democracy, like that of freedom and because it is basic to freedom, has to be reopened again and examined all over again. The word "planning" must have a modifier; it must be democratic planning or it is of small interest, neat and tidy though it may be.

But what is democratic planning? Are democracy and planning compatible? Are the two ideas feasible in this particular huge society? Certainly one would expect a few words on this subject in the two works discussed above; but other than some brief remarks of Dean Landis about the difficulty of those appointed to administrative agencies in keeping the public interest to the forefront of their consciousness, there is no consideration of the question. Nor is there much consideration of these questions elsewhere in official liberalism. The official liberal is marvelously adept at making blueprints for all of us, but when it comes to questions of the nature of parties, the power of private groups, the problems of participation, the role of government, and other such questions, he mainly falls back on a simple pluralism which with luck he hopes will solve all of those questions. Now, pluralism is a grand old doctrine and one would not give it up for the world, but unless it is defined with some precision as it would operate in the particular society of today and the particular society to come it is a way of avoiding problems.

Because official liberalism has not examined our power realities it cannot give adequate guidance to those problems and possibilities of freedom that so exercise the social critics. It has been unable to develop any concepts of change or political reality, to develop any image, theory, or vision of an on-

going developing society in which new forms of freedom
grow out of old. In fact, the future as postulated by official
liberalism, for all its sanitary comforts, is exactly present-day
American society rehoused, redistributed, reorganized, and re-
administered, but with all the activity taking place within the
same social framework, the same power structure, the same
value system, and all of it leaving freedom in its present position. The idea of a different society that will expand freedom,
make it more available to more people—this official liberalism
cannot offer to us.

If the planners are stuck fast in the upper world of bureaucratic insolence, the Marchers, the sit-in-ers, the direct actionists are stuck fast in the lower world of anarchic freedom. For
whatever cause they march, whether it be desegregation,
nuclear testing, peace, or other noble causes—and they are
noble causes—the gap between the Marcher and the upper
world is not only wide but widened farther by his very refusal
to play the game of politics or any other game belonging to
the upper world. Such statements are not to deny the impact
of the Marcher; indeed, his political and social impact has
been wider and more effective on a specific kind of issue than
any other organization in the past decade. And perhaps these
forms of direct action are all that is left to us today. But such
groups are limited by their nature as special-interest groups
(if one may be allowed to apply such an ugly and demeaning
terminology to what is after all not just direct action but
heroic action); their activity does nothing to touch the sources
of power of the bureaucrats. The tragedy of the loss of society
lies precisely in the gulf between the official liberal in the
White House, trapped into isolation by the system and out of
touch with the vital energies and aspirations of the real heroes
of America, the Marchers.

The saddest spectacle today is the gulf between those who

have the courage to protest and those of liberal persuasion who have the power to act but whose power is castrated by the game they must play with the bureaucrats of the upper world. The Marchers have discovered that freedom can be something other than personal autonomy; that it can mean participation in a group; that the act of participation in itself is a means of freedom; that it can be the invention of a new thing by a group and that the group itself is the source of this freedom; that it does not come simply from an acting-out of personal autonomy. The Marchers have shown that commitment to society makes possible a different dimension of freedom. But they march in the anarchy that a mass society allows and they do nothing to recognize that bureaucracy is an essential means to freedom. Nor do they do anything to change the basic realities of society, a point illustrated by a youth (white) who said in despair, "All right; so the Negro becomes desegregated. Swell. But then he becomes a dull bourgeois like the rest of us and joins the mass society."

The official liberal and the Marcher meet today only at the White House gates where the President sends his servant to provide them with hot coffee on a cold winter day. The loneliness of the White House, the difficulty it has in breaking through to the forces of freedom, were brought to a pitiful demonstration in that scene. Never was the gap between official liberal and Marcher, between the upper and lower worlds, so wide. And all the fault does not lie with the President.

Seldom have those who believe in freedom been so unable to tame and use power in its service. The official liberal is enmeshed in the games and follies and rituals of the upper world of bureaucracy and is increasingly impotent to drastically modify American society and to change its configuration of power. The Marcher is detached from effective social forms

of action and from the whole society of which he is perforce
a part and is increasingly impotent in affecting or even understanding the fundamental problem of freedom today. The
one cannot opt out of the game or break the rules on which its
useless tenure of power depends. The other foolishly thinks
that rules do not matter and that spontaneity and direct
action can become a substitute for the hard necessity of dealing with the reality of power and government. As the Marchers mill around outside the White House gates the big
decisions are made without them inside the gates. In the gap
between freedom languishes.

The issue of power is at the heart of the problem presented
by the loss of society. And the issue of power in turn intro-
duces the question of politics, democracy, and equality in
their relationship to freedom today.

6
The Loss of Politics

Given the political structure within which we must now act, I do not believe it is very likely that social scientists will become effective carriers of reason.

The facts about the newer means of history-making are a signal that men are not necessarily in the grip of fate, that men can now make history. But this fact is made ironic by the further fact that just now those ideologies which offer men the hope of making history have declined and are collapsing in the Western societies.

I do not know the answer to the question of political irresponsibility in our time. . . .

It is the political task of the social scientist—as of any liberal educator—continually to translate personal troubles into public issues, and public issues into terms of their human meaning for a variety of individuals.

C. WRIGHT MILLS*

The effect of the loss of history and society can be seen in the political situation. Politics is an essential factor in any valid concern with social questions. It is the means by which at least some part of a set of ideas intended to have a public effect can be made manifest, even if only through protest. It is the way our beliefs about society are embodied in the public arena and in the struggle for power.

Without politics such ideas, such beliefs, can be interesting and intellectually significant, but they remain private, technical, abstract, and irrelevant to power. Thus the discovery that cigarettes cause lung cancer will have at best a marginal effect

* C. Wright Mills, *The Sociological Imagination* (New York: Oxford University Press, 1959).

117

on public habits until it is sponsored as a political idea and until some group battles with the power of the advertisers who live off the death and ill-health of others. The power to change smoking habits necessarily involves a struggle for the power of some public agency that can bring about a change. And that struggle in turn demands not merely the assertion of scientific facts but the hand-to-hand battle with those who corrupt us.

Politics is not, therefore, simply one possible way of action for those who are concerned with public life; it is not simply an alternative that can be brought out of the closet on occasion whenever convenient. It is *the* way of action by which concern for public affairs defines and expresses itself. The essence of politics is found in the reach for instruments of affecting public behavior. Politics may be broadly defined to include an infinite number of activities, but they all have in common this desire for public power. If they cease to possess that desire, then they cease to be political and become something else—say, a philosophy.

Such concepts, which are truisms to political scientists, still have a capacity to surprise those sociologists who tend to confuse the reasons why people act in politics with what politics is about.[1] The politicization of a set of ideas in recent years has often seemed to be an "extra" that may or may not be advisable in a particular set of circumstances. No doubt the tactics of power-seeking demand special attention and often call for withdrawals as well as spectacular lunges forward. A "strategic retreat" is an honorable phrase to justify a recoupment after defeat in any form of combat. But tactics are not

[1] See Sidney Verba's excellent comment on the study of political behavior: ". . . though much is said on the various social and psychological influences that lead to a particular voting choice, there seems to be little concern over who won the election. . . ." "Political Behavior and Politics," *World Politics*, January, 1960.

in question. What is in question is the *necessity* to politicize
a set of ideas if they have a public aim or if they have a public
content and concern.

If ideas of public life die without politics, is the state of
their health dependent upon the state of their politics? Is it
necessary that they win, that they achieve their political goals,
for such ideas to exist?

To win is always pleasant and certainly victory revives and
stimulates. But there is no one-to-one ratio between the prospect of victory and the health of a set of ideas. Ideas can exist
as defeated for a long time and still be in a good state of health
as long as some political means are at hand and the political
act is not completely denied. Totalitarianism, correctly for its
purpose, tries to achieve the total denial of politics to its
opponents. Democracy, on the other hand, makes possible a
long continuance in defeat since the fluidity of its politics
always holds out some possibility of victory or partial success.
Just because the victors in a democratic society are never certain how long their victory will last or how sure their victory
is, just because one parliament cannot bind another, so the
defeated have possibilities before them if they wish to look
for them. Thus public ideas in a democracy can remain politi-
cized, even when the odds are heavily against them. Yet the
odds cannot be so heavily against them that no victory of any
kind is possible, for then politics would become a bitter joke.

For liberal thought the necessity of politicization is as absolute as it is for most doctrines of public affairs. But in its case
a special factor operates. Liberalism cannot exist as a doctrine
without the prospect of a successful politics because that is the
way freedom as the fundamental project of liberalism is postulated and achieved in a society. Others—the conservatives
in particular—aim to bring society to a standstill and hence
freedom to an end. For the conservative, politics is the art of

the dead end; it is the hope of bringing politics itself to a stop after society has achieved a state of plenitude of being, of stasis. To be antipolitical is natural and logical to a conservative. The liberal, however, must see politics not simply in instrumental terms but as the very process by which freedom within a society—as distinct from freedom in the private sphere—is made manifest. It then becomes not the art of achieving stasis but the art of social invention, a way by which a whole society can discover new social phenomena and thus find concrete means of using and experiencing freedom.

In a certain sense politics for a liberal is an art of the impossible, of creating what never existed before. It is not only a method by which problems are solved, by which reforms are achieved, although it is that. It is the continual possibility of achieving the new. One hastens to add that it can be a lot of other things too; e.g. a technique and means of corruption. But when it becomes those other things the liberal does not accept it; that is why corruption not only angers him in his pocketbook but disgusts him and often finds him naïve or surprised. *That* is not what *he* means by politics.

But while the liberal has a penchant for orderly, rational, and honest politics—a naïveté he will never outgrow—he can also recognize, when he is not despondent, that even the politics of corruption leave open certain possibilities other than the possibility that the corruption will grow worse. Maybe the corruption will be exposed! Indeed, the exposure of corruption is one of the favorite political activities of the liberal. Thus as long as there is a political life in which he can participate in some way, no matter how unsavory that political life may be, it can perform its function of offering concrete freedom to society and the individual, the chance to invent new forms of social order.

The politics in which the liberal must engage himself is

limited in aim and method no matter what the problem may be. As it is known today in the West, politics is a uniquely liberal method of discussion, pressure, and legalism through which development and change can be achieved. It is the only way the liberal knows. Except in his more ecstatic moments, and they are rare of late, he can only envisage change in his favor through the piecemeal, slow, and devious techniques of parliamentary politics of some kind or other. He is no millenarian. Big leaps forward frighten him more than they fascinate him. Sanity and ad hoc solutions are his prescriptions when things go awry.

When a "problem" arises it should be "studied" so that the "various avenues of approach" can be "postulated," preferably by a committee that will "bring together" the "various interests involved." Once we know "where we are" then a "method of action" can be "developed." Occasionally the liberal will look to "leadership" (the President is his favorite) as his "method of action" but even that particular way of "resolving" a situation can sometimes seem dangerous and risky, for leadership has a nasty way of degenerating into demogoguery, the very antithesis of politics. What liberal did not become, at times, suspicious of the melodious voice of Franklin Roosevelt? Thus the liberal is the political man par excellence. Without politics he is nowhere; he simply is not a liberal, or if that statement is considered too sweeping, he is a liberal operating under the most adverse circumstances. More accurately he is a liberal who cannot operate.

Liberalism is a public doctrine or it is nothing. It is not a doctrine of personal salvation like religion or a doctrine of scientific regeneration like Freudianism. It is focused squarely on public events and problems as they occur in the political life of a society and if it has nothing to say on those problems it has nothing to say on any problem.

Thus the cruelest dilemma of all for liberalism today. We have seen the despair with which the social critic looks at our society, and we have also seen his sense of bafflement as he looks at the prospects for change. In such a situation is politics still possible? If not, what are the consequences? If so, what kind of politics are possible?

Liberal Political Movements Since the War: the Ambiguity of Defeat

The question, Is liberal politics still possible? necessarily involves a consideration of such politics in the West since 1945.[2] If politics is still possible for the liberal, one aspect of that possibility must lie in the realm of current political movements that aim to capture the power of the state by winning elections (since he knows of no other way to capture that power). If a severe defeat has been sustained in the public arena by the liberal movements of today, a defeat that has all the characteristics of being a long-term and more or less permanent defeat, then this particular means of politics would have been put outside the boundary of possibility. The liberal has never liked to live in an ivory tower and he has always resented the slur that he does, that he, in contrast to the realistic conservative, does not know the tough, hard ways of politics in its everyday form of competition for power. He is

[2] Since this discussion will briefly broaden out to include the states of Western Europe and particularly Great Britain, a clarification of terminology is required. In Western Europe the word "liberal" still is used to mean the older liberalism of the nineteenth century, while in America it refers to a twentieth-century ideology that is not unrelated to nineteenth-century liberalism but that is distinctly unique and in conflict with it. Thus the equivalent groups in Western Europe are the "moderate" socialists. If a spectrum of of the "left" were established, it would run, reading from right to left, American liberal, moderate European socialist, left-wing European socialist. All of these are subsumed here under the heading "liberal" on the basis that the differences between them are less than the differences between them as a group and nineteenth-century liberalism whether in America or Europe.

right to resent that slur and, it might be added, there is no one who can be meaner in politics than a liberal with an ideological glint in his eye. One may pity the conservative or anyone else who crosses the path of the liberal in search of purity.

In pursuit not necessarily of purity but of the power to establish policies in the interest of his version of the good life, the liberal has in fact throughout his history created an impressive array of political parties and a widespread network of pressure groups. Any thought that he has been an ineffective underdog in the realm of twentieth-century politics can be dismissed out of hand. True he has often lost, and he has lost some very important battles: e.g., the fight against fascism in the 1930's, although in the 1940's a costly victory was eventually achieved. And while the range and spectrum of policies and groups involved in his political effort have been wide and even sometimes eccentric it has on the whole been consistent and purposeful. The very fervor of the conservative counterattack in recent years has been testimony to the political success of the liberal in the past. It is not too much to say, indeed, that from about 1890 a liberal political offensive of vast dimensions established both the main political and ideological approaches that have become characteristic of Western society and, in some nations at least, created the main legal, bureaucratic, and structural forms of twentieth-century society and state.

In doing so, liberalism gave the impression to itself as well as to those who opposed it that it was the aggressive and uniquely qualified expression and representative of the century, that liberal political movements were, even when defeated, the appointed vessel of history. This assumption was possible and necessary because it was manifest that its conservative opposition had nothing to contribute to the problems that clearly and unmistakably faced twentieth-century society. When liberal political movements claimed to be the only movements that could operate modern society they were not far wrong.

They were not far wrong because they were brilliantly suited to dragging the society of the time away from the most vicious habits of the nineteenth century—and we sometimes forget how vicious that century could be—into a more humane way of life in the twentieth. Liberalism in the West originated as a way of rectifying the wrongs of the nineteenth century and of finding a new society to take its place. In doing so, it established a new social morality and a new expectation of what the state and those who hold power are expected to do. This effort provided a worthy focus through the first half of the twentieth century. Liberal political parties and movements knew what they wanted and were able to develop policies that postulated precise forms of governmental action and that could take form in legislative enactment and bureaucratic manipulation.

The question the liberal must face today in the political arena is whether this role is played out and, if it is, whether his criticism of society is such that another form of liberal politics can emerge. And that question must be put in the context of the political defeats that have piled up on liberalism since 1950.

A *tour d'horizon* will indicate that these defeats are not normal ups and downs, are not a downward zig which will be replaced by an upward zag, but that they are defeats that have accompanied a fundamental change in Western political life. This change derives from the era of good-feeling that followed the crises of the first years after World War II and that accompanied the increasing prosperity of the fifties in Europe as well as America. It was at this time that the liberal found himself dished by the conservatives who now took to the achievements of liberalism and made them their own without at the same time affecting the free enterprise or class-status system. The sophistication with which this was done varied from one state to another; in Great Britain it was done with great sophistication, in America it was done without sophistication, and in France it was done brutally. Some liberals became so confused by this situation that they actually began to talk about the "end of ideology," exactly, of course, the kind of talk the conservatives wished to foster. What group would not want their opposition to believe that there was no longer an ideological struggle? But ideological issues were in fact as lively as ever. What had changed was not the ideological nature of politics but the context in which an ideological conflict or any conflict could be developed and sustained.

The politics of accommodation has always been a significant function of the political system of Western democracy and especially of America. It is excellently designed for a social and political system that is both pluralistic and prosperous. It is conceived for non-crisis situations; where there is no open crisis one thing can be accommodated to another without much consideration for what it is that is being accommodated. The object is to make the system "work"; i.e., to keep the social world that exists going not necessarily without change but without basic change. The politics of accommodation does not make pronouncements on basic problems. As long as "the system," however it may be defined, "works," then all is well. The politics of accommodation is a system designed to perpetuate system qua system.

It is also calculated to drive the liberal wild. Not only does it confuse his sense of ideological identity; more important, the political system suddenly seems hopeless, uninteresting, and futile.

It seems to be all of those things because of the conflict be-

tween the liberal desire for change and his need for qualitative discriminations on the one hand, and on the other the
system's difficulty in either achieving important change or
making qualitative discriminations. We have seen the depth
of the liberal's conviction today, as expressed by the social
critics, that he is in the hands of a society dedicated to the
rejection of freedom or at least to ignoring it. We have also
seen that it is not a matter of partial criticism of society, of
attack on this evil or that, but of total criticism, which views
each part of society as indicative of the whole. Such criticisms
make demands on the politics of accommodation that it cannot meet.

During crisis conditions, the system of accommodation can
either be suspended or work with enough flexibility to meet
some of the most important liberal criticisms. But in non-
crisis conditions, in an era of good feelings and prosperity, the
system accommodates itself to everything but the liberal desire to make important changes, to get something done. In
these circumstances the system takes on the appearance of im-
movability, of rigidity, which becomes the despair of the liberal. The play of forces between Congress and President,
between Parliament and Prime Minister, between National
Assembly and either or both Prime Minister and President,
no longer seem to the liberal to give an entrance into power
or influence but to become simply a play without meaning
and climax. Political transcendence hardly seems feasible
under such circumstances.

For the liberal, a politics that does not provide transcendence is not one that engages his interest or passion. In this
situation he is defeated by the gap between his desire for
fundamental social change—a desire for even more fundamental change than in a time of crisis when his concern is to
keep society afloat—and the general social sense of well-being

that comes from prosperity and good feelings, from the lack of a crisis. While his fellowmen are supposedly happy and contented, the liberal is uncomfortably aware of basic weaknesses and threats in his society.

Thus the social critic is trapped by an ambiguous defeat. Society allows and even encourages him to work hard at attack on the social system yet nothing happens and the critic cannot tell what it is that defeats him because there is no particular enemy in sight. How can there be since no one opposes him? The only effect his attacks have on the system is to create a market for social criticism and to make money for the author which, pleasant though it is, is not what he meant at all. More and more he finds himself being paid to attack the system, and all the while it grows stronger, thus enabling him to derive even more financial benefit from the attacks. To be sure, such a situation is humorous, but one can readily understand the sense of political ambiguity, not to mention frustration, that it must cause. One is either serious or one is not; one is either honest or one is not. But in these circumstances one cannot be serious, and one finds it increasingly difficult to be honest.

Social criticism is not written to make money; it is written —as one practitioner said in a different time—to change the world. If one can change the world and make money, well and good; but just to make money . . . ! Just to gain fame . . . ! Up to now social criticism, ideology, social philosophy, call it what you will, has had some role, however small it may have been, as a catalyst of change and development. But now it turns out to be, sadly, most sadly . . . therapy! Everything is absorbed; everything is conjured with; everything finds its place in the going system. And everything, including one's most cherished, serious, and honest beliefs, becomes a farce. It all ends up on an Open End and the David Susskinds of this world drink it all in, solemnly and without harm; the open end becomes the bottomless pit. Everything is said, but not only does nothing happen; it is clear that nothing will happen. Where, now, is the good old liberal belief that "ideas are weapons" (to quote a title from long ago)? Ideas are not weapons; they are counters in the game of money and academic prestige, and social theory is simply used to make the reader in his glassy suburb realize that his neighbor is in the same mess that he is except that one's neighbor is in a slightly worse mess because he has not yet read the latest book attacking himself. He soon will, however.

Ambiguity is a mild word for the feeling of rage and outrage that seizes the critic at this point of the game. Instead of social philosophy leading to a politics of action, it leads to television appearances. (And if one refuses the television appearance, then one is, of course, counted Out.) There is no defeat because there is no confrontation. It is not only an open end; it is a dead end. Politics in such a situation becomes futile because the system has infinite capabilities for the absorption of foreign matter.

The second source of ambiguous defeat lies in the doubts the liberal has acquired since 1939 about the state in general and the welfare state in particular. Here the ambiguity comes from the fact of defeat by the liberal's own chosen instrument. He does not deny, of course, that the welfare state is better than no welfare state, that action by the state to eradicate wrongs and social grievances and to solve social problems is better than no action. But the experience of the crudeness and tyranny of state action even in democracies has warned him of the freedom that can be lost through the agency of the state. At the same time he has also come to realize that even when the state does not oppress it is, in the modern bureaucratic world, under the best of circumstances, a distant and manipulative instrument, and that a society organized under the aegis of the state is hardly the best way to achieve human brotherhood.

A sort of mild anarchism has crept into liberalism as it has watched with some consternation how the state gathers more and more power to itself. The state is increasingly seen as a way of avoiding human responsibility; the system of representation in a democratic society is increasingly seen as divorced from reality. At best the state no longer appears to solve the fundamental issues of society. At worst it may make it impossible to solve fundamental issues and may rob the individual of his abilities and obligation to act. The basic weapon of the liberal in the political scene no longer seems to be quite so innocent as it once was. Certainly, it offers no panacea, no positively correct methods or solutions. Such disenchantment has been especially potent in Great Britain—from which it has spread to America—where the nationalization of industry is now more and more a mockery. Whatever the nationalization of industry achieved it was not the social revolution that was once assumed to be its consequence.

The ambiguity of this situation lies in the fact that, with all its faults, the state is still the only means at hand for dealing with the problems of a large, complex, and advanced society despite the fact that the liberal is left with a gnawing sense of defeat when state action becomes successful and habitual. Today a politics dedicated to more schemes for state intervention can draw only the mildest enthusiasm; such schemes may be necessary but a jaundiced awareness of the limits of state action is the best hope the liberal can summon. Is television bad, the scourge of our time? Assuredly it is, but does one want the FCC to take it in hand? Perhaps, but the answer is faint and dubious. Yet what else can be suggested? Evangelical conversion on the part of television owners and producers? Or should the liberal simply ignore television and all the muck it throws on the American people? If he does he is indeed contracting away from politics and from society itself.

Finally, there is the ambiguity that arises from the liberal's uncertain sense of having been defeated by democracy. Indeed, the problem is: *Has* he been defeated? The puzzle that democracy in our era presents to the liberal lies deep in the failure of democratic politics to be democratic in any sense that he expected. Here is a people, here are societies, that have finally freed themselves from the grip of material necessity for the first time in history. Never have so many owed so little to so few; and yet in France the many hand over their democratic rights to a quasi-monarch, in Great Britain they scramble for the products of the idiot box, and in America they allow themselves to be converted from The People into The Other-Directed. Is that what the struggle for universal suffrage was about?!

What is at fault, the idea that The People can rule themselves or some malign force which is corrupting the individual? Undoubtedly the latter. Undoubtedly? Hopefully, perhaps, the latter. For the brutal fact of the matter is that The People have not used the resources of a democratic state to free themselves. In this connection it is well to point out that in America the most revolutionary and democratic actions in the past decade have not come from The People's representatives, congressmen, or President, but from, of all places, the Supreme Court. The Supreme Court, the apostle of democracy! It is an awesome sight, certainly, for democracy to be rescued by the Supreme Court, for the Supreme Court to do what The People acting through their representatives could not do, but it is hardly conducive to faith in democratic politics.

The liberal has not lost his belief in democracy; he could never do that and still be a liberal. But he cannot prevent a note of doubt from creeping into his discussion of democracy. The People? "Ah yes; well, the problem is more complicated than one had thought. First of all," he will explain with a cough of deprecation, "there are all these groups; The People, you see, are not really The People, they are groups of people really, suburbanites, upper income, and all that. Then there are these elites; now these elites, they must be carefully considered." The analysis becomes increasingly finespun, and as one writer has put it, "Two cheers for democracy," or another, what we have is a "semisovereign people."

Well and good. Refined analysis is better than naïveté. Yet a refined theory of democratic politics has yet to be established in the place of the old naïveté. Equally important, the possibility of the liberal making his way in democratic politics is obscured by the meaning of the defeats he sustains there. Are they defeats that result from some profound weakness of democracy itself, or are they defeats due to the lack of sufficient democracy? The question is still open.

The ambiguities that the liberal meets in the political arena today have weakened his confidence in the political process as a means of resolving his problems. They have done more. They have made him into something very close to an apolitical animal. A brief consideration of the concepts put forward by the social critics concerning the nature of the American political system will show the extent to which they have rejected politics as a means of influencing the society in which they must live.

The Refusal of Politics

The refusal of politics by the social critics takes two forms. It is the refusal to consider politics at all. Or it is the refusal to see that politics can offer any solutions to problems that are

seen as possessing sociological rather than political dimensions. Despite their different stance these attitudes come to
the same result, a refusal of politics as a means to liberal ends,
a refusal to take politics seriously. Politics is seen to be part
and parcel of the social forces at work in the rest of the society
and therefore contaminated and incapable of transcendence,
of providing a means of change.

It is one of the problems of general theory that subsumes a
whole society under its analysis that once the whole society is
condemned no one part of it can escape condemnation.
Theory is, of course, of the essence. But the contingent needs
to be considered too. It is a grand thing to encompass a whole
society in terms of character types and to bundle a whole
political system into the same holistic bag; or to end all political issues with the majestic sweep of a slogan such as "the
power elite"; or to condemn the whole moral existence of a
nation by referring to it as "absurd." But not only is the
approach that underlies such conclusions of dubious scientific
worth—general theories as such are not the main concern of
scientists, it should be noted—the rigidity that results from
such theories is a positive hindrance to the solution of the
very problem that the analysis itself reveals. To give up scientific problem-solving for unscientific general theories is indeed to make a bad trade. The desire to be the Freud of the
social sciences is a hard one for social scientists today to resist.
But the assumption that underlies this desire and that is
found in most social criticism today, namely, that to discover
the secret springs of action and behavior in a society will lead
it to transcendence via the couch of the social critics is, as we
have seen, intellectually fallacious. It simply leads to a dead-
end trap where society as patient and social critic as analyst
give each other the comfort of self-exposure.

Thus the fate of politics in the hands of American social

critics. For them politics has ceased to be a way of acting on specific ills of a society because it is itself one of the key symptoms.

So hopeless does politics seem to some social critics that they can condemn a whole society and hardly mention politics. Neither William Whyte, Jr., in *The Organization Man* nor Paul Goodman in *Growing Up Absurd*—two books that are in many ways at opposite poles from each other—give sustained, serious, or even intelligent consideration to the American political system in their condemnation of society. The solutions of both critics to the problems that haunt them— and haunt is the word—are, to say the least, therefore eccentric and without much relevance. Indeed, in the absence of a discussion of politics it is difficult to know if they have any solutions to offer or whether instead we are not just being given a good moral shaking.

If David Riesman and C. Wright Mills have the wisdom to discuss politics rather than assume its absence, their analysis does not move us much further. Riesman and Mills describe American politics in almost exactly opposite terms, yet the net result is, oddly, not very different. Riesman sees politics in terms of veto groups, of groups that share power rather than dominate and thus that not only restrict their own power but the power of everyone else. This analysis, which, of course, has long been commonplace among political scientists and which has a long history in political theory, is derived by Riesman from his more general analysis of the sociological and characterological features of America; it acquires its main significance from the sociological underpinning of its commonplaceness rather than from its inherent originality. Politics is, in this kind of general theory, a derivative of characterological types rather than an independent phenomenon with its own rules of activity and its own particular effects. This being the case, Riesman's view on politics is simply that veto politics is a function of other-direction. Hence in a very real sense he can be said not to discuss politics at all, for his interest in the subject, he tells us in *The Lonely Crowd*, is centered "like that of many people today . . . not so much on the political sphere itself as on the process by which people become related to it. . . ."[3] or: "We shall regard politics as one of the spheres in which inner-directed and other-directed people carry out their respective rounds of life and encounter each other in antagonistic or symbiotic fashion—as a sphere, that is, of characterological struggle."[4]

Such a ruthless disregard for what politics is about—namely, the struggle over power and the ends of power—is a facet of the liberal himself as other-directed. It is *he* who has become so aware of other peoples' opinions of himself that he can no longer see politics as having any other significance than that of "style." Thus Riesman sees politics as an arena that is dominated by the "indignants" (the moralizing inner-directed) or the "inside-dopester," who tries to defend himself by operating inside the game of politics rather than by the use of moral attitudes, since his object is to be passive rather than involved in such attitudes. The result of this dualism is a system of politics by veto groups, which represents a shift from moralizing to tolerance: ". . . veto groups are neither leader groups nor led-groups. . . . Both within the groups and in the situation created by their presence, the political mood tends to become one of other-directed tolerance. . . . By their very nature the veto groups exist as defence groups, not as leadership groups."[5]

There is, of course, point to this description of politics in our time. But its most significant aspect is the refusal of poli-

[3] Riesman, *The Lonely Crowd*, p. 178.
[4] *Ibid.*, p. 183.
[5] *Ibid.*, pp. 244, 245.

tics that such an analysis involves.[6] It is a refusal not in the
sense of approval; quite the contrary, Riesman emphatically
disapproves and would escape from it through the personal
autonomy we have already discussed. But it is a refusal in the
sense of not considering politics as an independent force that
stimulates change. To Riesman politics is conceivable only in
terms of a dualism between morality and tolerance. Thus he
cannot look upon it as posing problems that call for appropriate political acts. Riesman imprisons politics in a dualism and
then announces triumphantly that politics is hopeless and that
we must turn to personal autonomy. One can only agree that
politics as he describes it is indeed hopeless. Fortunately what
he has described is not politics at all but only the result of a
refusal to describe it.

The possibility that some liberals today are more interested
in sociological general theory than in political data gains increased support when the views of C. Wright Mills on the
subject are considered. Where Riesman sees that power is so
dispersed that it cannot be made effective, Mills sees power
as so concentrated that nobody but a small elite can possess
and participate in a politics that is now reserved exclusively
for the power elite. What Riesman describes as veto groups
is what Mills calls the middle levels of politics, which are
subordinate to the upper level and of little operational importance. Politicians, Mills announces, are no longer significant. And the theory of a balance of forces in American
politics is no longer applicable. Thus: "In so far as the structural clue to the power elite today lies in the political order,
that clue is the decline of politics as genuine and public debate of alternative decisions. . . ."[7] Politics, to Mills, is a façade

---

[6] John Kenneth Galbraith has pointed out that social criticism should be
directed toward the achievement of political change: "For those who seek
change, criticism is an essential instrument of political action." *Atlantic
Monthly*, February, 1962.

[7] Mills, *The Power Elite*, p. 274.

behind which the power elite operates. What we have today is
a system in which there "are no national parties . . . which by
their debate focus national issues clearly and responsibly and
continuously."[8] Since no Western and democratic society ever
has possessed such parties or is likely to, and since the closest
approximation is the British party system, which has demonstrated such abysmal failures in the twentieth century compared to the American party system, it seems a little hard on
the part of Mills to use such a standard to judge American
politics. But such standards are not only typical of the incompetence of the social critic in the field of politics; it is also
a useful standard for Mills, since his catastrophism requires
that politics be shown to be ineffective at best or corrupt at
worst.

Both Riesman and Mills deny the validity of politics as a
means of action by showing that it offers not even the possibility of solutions to any important problem. No doubt American politics displays to a high degree, much too high a degree,
many of the characteristics they attribute to it. But to treat
politics as a function or derivative of a fancy sociological
theory is not to take it seriously.

The refusal to consider politics as a means to the solution
of the problems of a society, as possessing the potentiality of
transcendence, may or may not be correct; certainly there are
real reasons for fearing that the political life of America today
is flaccid and incapable of attack on the threats to freedom,
even though, as we shall see, there are also some grounds for a
less pessimistic analysis. But what is astounding is the way in
which this type of liberal thinking has cut itself off in the interest of general theory from the possibilities that politics
should and might possess for liberal aims.

[8] *Ibid.*, p. 254.

The Transformation of Liberalism

The refusal of politics by the social critics parallels the transformation of liberalism, which has occurred because the liberal cannot see any way to bridge the gap between the upper and lower worlds. The transformation of liberalism lies in accepting the split between the official liberal and those who find it necessary to work for freedom within the relatively unstructured situation that exists outside the formal political system. The latter draw their rationale from the refusal of politics promulgated by the social critics. Accordingly, liberalism has in a very real sense gone underground, where it operates within the realm of personal responsibility and where it has been transformed into a personal commitment, an existentialist act.

In some ways it is none the worse for such a development. It is what liberalism has always been or should have been, and what politics has sometimes disguised under the façade of organization. Such a transformation can, of course, create some literally excruciating moral and personal dilemmas for the individual as he faces the upper world alone or in a small and weak group, but the liberal conscience glories in self-examination and moral dilemmas and usually arises from the process toughened and more firmly committed. Organizational and large-scale politics can easily mask the immediacy and anguish of concrete problems under a haze of rhetoric and self-satisfaction. It is not as easy to be a liberal by oneself as it is to be a liberal as a member of a large and successful political movement. Nor is it as easy to be a liberal now as it was in the 1930's when it was the obvious thing to be.

It is, nevertheless, a great change from the idea that liberalism could operate with some success in the political institutions that it had helped create, work, and reform. It is therefore necessary to ask what kind of politics is feasible for the liberal in the lower world of anarchic freedom. The most important answer is found in the "force of nonviolence," a phrase which makes it clear that the liberal in this situation recognizes his distance from the forces of violence, that is, power. The philosophy of nonviolence in America today, as explained by one of its interpreters,[9] would move the liberal away from the sterility of doing nothing but complain. Instead of accepting personal autonomy as the end object and as an ultimate statement of what the liberal can achieve today, nonviolence aims to use it to take advantage of whatever political and social possibilities are available to the powerless. If nonviolence is not pressed to its absolute conclusion of total passivity it can produce some degree of social change. The desegregation movement has shown (once again; earlier reform movements have also used its methods) the possibility of using "minimum force to achieve maximum justice." Nonviolence from this point of view may be generalized into a theory to be applied to social problems other than desegregation, so that it becomes a technique of social change in a time when the normal political institutions of society seem unable to move. It is a technique of forcing issues without directly confronting the upper world of bureaucratic insolence, a confrontation that would end in defeat since it controls power. It is "guerilla warfare in time of peace." This description of what is implicit in the most successful and alive aspect of liberal politics in the last half-decade demonstrates what liberalism has come to mean in the underground. The liberal today has had to recognize that the legitimate political system is at best only one focus of his activity and that he is on his

---

[9] Howard Zinn in his interesting and important essay "The Force of Nonviolence," *The Nation*, March 17, 1962.

own outside the realms of political parties, legislatures, and even to some extent the law.

But even though it is necessary to recognize the usefulness of this approach, it is also necessary to consider that such politics can only be one focus of the liberal's political commitment because this difficult stance does not make good the loss of politics. Indeed, it can even be viewed as the institutionalization of the loss of politics. For liberal politics to take this form is of necessity to limit itself to the lowest and most rudimentary political life and thought. In the practical sphere of activity this implies that it will remain inchoate and diffuse and that it will continue to be the vehicle of special, single-issue groups fighting for their specific programs and in the process submerging and ignoring anything wider than their own programs. Purposive change will occur as a result of these struggles and bureaucratic insolence will sustain some important defeats. But the implications of those defeats will not become clear even to those responsible for them and such victories will be diffused and absorbed into contradictory currents or perhaps simply into backwaters of stagnation.

In this situation liberalism will continue to be a matter of personal protest resting upon the choice of an individual or small unprotected groups. Such protest will repeat and perhaps develop the insights of social criticism, but the intellectual content of both will continue to be focused around the problems of personal conduct in the face of a society that the social critic has taught the liberal to despise. Hence as he withdraws into his special-issue group in the practical sphere, so will he withdraw into his personal autonomy in the intellectual sphere. Social criticism will be his justification for this withdrawal, since in our time it can be defined as the ideology of liberalism in an era of withdrawal from society.

7

The Coming Search for Freedom

Communism has become a serious threat to Western civilization chiefly because the West lost control of the great processes of political, economic, and technological change which—partly through its virtues and partly through its shortcomings—the West itself had initiated.

JAMES WARBURG*

Certain American elite groups have chosen the road of "inner emigration," retreating from social responsibilities into, at best, a concern with their immediate surroundings, family, and friends. . . . The fact that they remain without political purpose beyond their small civic circles limits their vision and hence their growth.

DAVID RIESMAN and MICHAEL MACCOBY*

Why has liberalism come to the point of pessimistic exhaustion? What possibilities are there that the liberal may become a useful social animal who finds his personal scope within society rather than apart from it? As we have seen, the social critics have created a new search for freedom which is characterized by pessimism and flight from history, society, and politics. In so doing, however, they have filled an important function in orienting liberalism toward the new conditions of today and making it understood that new problems have arisen to take the place of the old. They have at least sought the idea of freedom at this particular point in time. Is it possible to see on the horizon another search for freedom—one

* In *The Liberal Papers,* edited by James Roosevelt (Chicago: Quadrangle Books, 1962).

that will be a commitment to society—and to feel at least a twinge of optimism?

The Exhaustion of Liberal Energies and the Mood of the Fifties

The social critics have risen to prominence since the appearance of Riesman's *The Lonely Crowd* in 1950. Their works form a genre typical of the fifties, a decade of consolidation that refused adventure. It was a period when the unfolding processes of history apparently came to an end. A halt had been called—not a return to normalcy nor an advance to a new future. Its main object was to let the individual find his own recreation. He was allowed the personal freedom to enjoy himself, while society functioned simply as an economic organ, producing goods for the individual to consume. Politics offered either the disgusting spectacle of the buffoon trying to take over the state or the reluctant executive fumbling his lines.

Before 1950, America had been through some twenty years of creative effort, during which time it had made world history as never before and had become the center of world power. It had not only made its own history but had done so for others as well. During those same years, America had changed its domestic face so radically that by 1950 it was impossible to think realistically of returning to the conditions that obtained before 1929. Though not militantly interventionist, the government could no longer be conceived as unconcerned with what happened in society or to the economy.

By 1950 it was time to rest. More: it was hard to know what else had to be done. All that seemed necessary was to administer better that which seemed to be fairly well administered. This was not complacency; everyone on all sides and with

much solemnity agreed that great problems existed everywhere. It was, however, refusal—the refusal to meet those
problems with new ways of social action. There was a plethora
of new techniques, but a paucity of change in society. Whatever dynamic forces were at work were not allowed to emerge
as history-making forces or as forces that could shape politics
and society. Change became an irrelevance.

The social critics reflect this era in their despair at its failure and meaninglessness but also and most importantly in
their fundamental acceptance of its postulates. The exhaustion of American creativity in the realm of social and political
change is the basic datum from which they start. It is the most
remarkable fact they see about their time. Where other and
earlier commentators about society had been most impressed
with, say, the creative possibilities inherent in the exploitation of the proletariat, or in the conflicts between capital and
labor, the social critics were most impressed with the fact that
this was a society that had lost its ability to create new forms
of social activity and action. They saw the threat that this
posed to freedom. But they also had to accept the lack of
creativity as a reality. To them society was exactly this crushing of creativity. Their theories had to prove, therefore, why
the society of today destroyed creativity and why it established
conformity. History, society, and politics were no longer the
producers of conflict; rather, conflict, if it existed at all, must
come from outside those areas, must exist independently of
anything but itself. Society had become such a deadening
thing that it could not even produce a conflict within itself
that might break the cake of conformity enclosing it. The very
condition of America in the 1950's that produced this view
prevented the social critics from inventing the means of transcending it and hence made them into logical representatives
of their historical environment. They were the liberal mind

of the 1950's as it came to a recognition of what the 1950's were.

The paralysis of the period was one immediate source of the loss of history, society, and politics. The other source was the problem of communism, which emerged into the full light of day at that time. The problem posed by communism for America in those years was twofold. First, it was a threat to American values. Second, it became manifest that it had not failed in terms of its own values and objectives and that it was here to stay.

As a result of an exposure to and experience of an earlier totalitarianism, the American liberal as well as the American conservative in the 1950's grasped only too well the fact of a common enemy outside the gates. In the face of that enemy the liberal was pressed into an alliance with his opponents in domestic politics. He found it difficult to attack his new ally and to create a politics of conflict. It was a time of the vital center. Because the communist issue took precedence over all other issues and dominated almost all policy, the liberal found it increasingly difficult to find an independent role for himself in politics. It was without doubt the greatest trick the conservative had ever played on him. But the liberal had helped the conservative to play the trick by accepting too readily at the beginning of the decade the latter's definition of what the world crisis was about.

And once the trick was played it was hard to regain the ground lost. When communism became the only "real" issue, anything that did not fit into a black-and-white politics was ignored. The liberal did not, of course, have much choice since he did not control any effective organs of public opinion, and, more important, because he could not help but agree that communism was in fact the fundamental problem of his time. Whatever the cause of this stultifying situation, when

American politics became solely the story of "how to fight communism," liberalism came to an end as an active political force. Though the liberal in fact weakly tried to prevent anti-communism from becoming the only issue, insofar as it blanketed all others he was counted out in political life.

The success of communism, the dynamics of its thrust, or, more accurately, the seeming dynamics of its thrust, also posed a special problem for the democratic values held by the liberal. He saw plainly, and quite correctly, that the conservative had no answer to the threat of an expanding communism. But it was also clear that a liberalism on the defensive had little to contribute that was dynamic and capable of acting as a counterthrust. Whatever liberalism was in this period, it was not dynamic. Indeed, if it could preserve its own existence it was doing well. In the late 1940's liberalism had shown a spirit of dynamic counterthrust; the Marshall Plan and foreign aid in general succeeded in reorienting American policy so that at least some kind of effective foreign policy was at hand. The Marshall Plan in particular was an imaginative and fruitful concept in which the idea of a new type of government action in a new field of endeavor was derived from a marriage of the liberal belief in pragmatic governmental intervention in economic activity and the facts of foreign affairs. Yet with the coming of the 1950's the liberal response along with everyone else's became more and more stereotyped and less and less dynamic. The existence of an administration devoted to stereotyped activity aided the weakening of the liberal response to communism. Even the liberal, therefore (in the person of Adlai Stevenson), began to worry about "the national purpose." But what is worry about "the national purpose" but a recognition that there is no national purpose? What is it but the recognition that there is a loss of dynamic answer to a dynamic enemy? For the liberal the sneaking suspicion that the communist was dynamic and himself inert was one of the most frustrating and devastating fears of the period. His failure not only to have a "solution" for Cuba but even to know what to think about it is simply one dramatic example of a more general sense of impotence. On such subjects liberalism was tongue-tied.

The writings of the social critics mirror the sense that more dynamic movements are abroad than liberalism by their inability to see it as anything more than a defense against the threats that surround it. Freedom, as we have seen, is conceived by the social critics as something existing in the undergrowth. It certainly is not portrayed as the solvent of the world's troubles or of anybody's troubles. Indeed, if it is so difficult for the American to achieve freedom, it would seem that the ability of other peoples outside the United States to achieve it is almost nil. Certainly no one, and least of all the liberal, believes that liberalism has much relevance today for the backward states. At the most it offers technical solutions with a tinge of liberal values added. Constitutionalism—to choose one of the favorite devices of the liberal mind—is hardly feasible or useful in the backward areas. And the education of the many, to choose another liberal tenet, we know now leads only to a revolutionary elite and makes more feasible the coming of a communist tyranny. And so it goes. Liberalism may survive in America, but it hardly seems to be the wave of the future outside of America. In such a situation the liberal may try to bring rationality into a situation by an Alliance for Progress, but he is soon brought to realize that the lack of rationality is precisely the key trait of a backward state. David Riesman makes the point when he observes of the underdeveloped areas: "Certainly, inventions worked out in the West, such as federalism and judicial protection of minority rights (which offer bulkheads against bigotry in America), seem of scant possibility when ethnic blocs and religious sects, newly armed with slogans and the power to harm, struggle at once to establish an identity and to mark its boundaries. Thus, while we can prefigure the end of tradition, it is hard to envisage the beginning of enlightenment."[1] At one time, before the disillusionments of the fifties, liberal government was the accepted model for government. Today the best that can be hoped for is that it will arrive at the end of a long and bloody road. The loss of a hopeful future the liberal feels in domestic affairs he feels even more intensely when he looks outside his own country.

To some degree the sense of impotence expressed by the social critics is related to the particular history of the generation that wrote the social criticism of the fifties. Whatever their own personal experiences—and nothing is suggested here concerning those experiences—they are representative in point of age of that group that was badly burned by communism. It is no coincidence that social criticism came to the fore at a time when the many intellectuals were trying to work out their guilt complexes over their flirtations with communism and with having failed earlier to discover its threat. Those liberals who came of political age in the 1930's and 1940's rightly or wrongly, and more often wrongly, in the 1950's looked back over their past to evaluate what they had done and not done in their earlier years. Their evaluation found its counterpart and justification in the ideas of social criticism. Whatever mistakes had been made could be put aside by the adoption of this philosophy of social quietism, by the rejection of history, and by cynicism about politics. Revulsion against being "had," or having been made a fool of in more naïve times, was characteristic of this group.

[1] David Riesman in his introduction to Daniel Lerner's *The Passing of Traditional Society* (New York: The Free Press of Glencoe, 1958), pp. 6-7.

Thus in the fifties the domestic history of America and the seeming dynamic qualities of communism combined to produce the exhaustion of liberal energies. Liberalism became unsure of itself and defensive; the world no longer seemed to have a place for it. Instead, history, society, and politics seemed to be moving away from liberalism, leaving it stranded as a historical phenomenon of the past—a past that had also become increasingly dubious. There seemed to be little work that liberalism could perform. It could be held as a personal faith. But as a movement of opinion that energized a given political situation it had virtually ceased to exist. The idea that liberalism was a driving force determining the future and bringing about new experiences of freedom through social innovation was no longer feasible. Instead it became in large part an act of social criticism that terrified itself by its own descriptions of the threats that a new society had created. Hagridden by its own doubts, it ceased to believe in the possibility of transcending its situation, though it yearned for transcendence as never before.

The End of Liberal Self-Effacement?

Fortunately liberalism has a certain reservoir of ebullience that runs deep even as it goes underground in periods of futility. If nothing else, the liberal tends to get bored with prospects of doom; in this he differs fundamentally, one might add, from the conservative, who endlessly enjoys forecasts of doom and cannot exist without them. Having passed through his period of catharsis and self-effacement—having proved that his situation is impossible and that all avenues are closed —the liberal in the first years of the 1960's began to show signs of reviving his sense of the pragmatic in place of wallowing in the doldrums of sociological theory. In part this was and is a response to the success of the integration movement qua movement which showed that acts of protest could exist and have an impact. In part it was a response to the spirit of the liberal college student who does not carry the burdens of the older generation and who is capable of absorbing the insights of social criticism without letting them destroy his energies. But in part it is due, too, to the realization among the leading social critics themselves that liberalism is not only social theory but a means of confronting social, historical, and political reality by working within the concrete problems of our time.

Paul Goodman, David Riesman, and C. Wright Mills in the early 1960's each in their own way tried to face the problem stated by Goodman in his *Utopian Essays and Practical Proposals:* "The present crisis in which an American writes is a peculiar one. He confronts in his audience the attitude that things are well enough, there is nothing to be grievous or angry about, and anyways our situation is inevitable. . . . At the same time, these same people are evidently in the grip of anxiety in the face of changes that they don't begin to prepare for. Instead they eat up books that glumly expose our plight. . . ."[2] Goodman has now begun to talk to these people by showing how change can be controlled by rationality and will. He tells them what they should be doing; for example, to ban cars from Manhattan or to improve the environment for youth through work camps and better vocational guidance. He also tells them that utopianism is simply "common sense and direct action toward obvious goods. . . ." Against this utopian way of thinking he poses the inadequacy of "our present 'organized' procedures [which] are simply not good enough to cope with our technological changes." Goodman

[2] Paul Goodman, *Utopian Essays and Practical Proposals* (New York: Random House, Inc., 1962), p. xvi.

is now bent on teaching in a concrete way what can be done to improve human existence in the United States of the 1960's and on showing that coping is possible. His main aim is not to describe a situation of absurdity but to move men out of it by getting them to work on detailed and particular problems. It is the same object that motivates his *Community of Scholars* (1962), where he describes a university as a community of scholars in conflict and confrontation with society, an emphasis on a "conflictal" community that is also found in *Utopian Essays and Practical Proposals*. In all his suggestions for specific change Goodman has been at pains not simply to be relevant in the sense of showing what must and can be done but to make clear that action must take place in a realistic framework of conflict within a particular society over particular objects. One may or may not agree with his particular proposals—although they are in fact commonsensical—but one must recognize that his insistence on what is possible now, in this society, will help open up a different way of thinking about the situation of freedom in our time than that represented by social criticism.

David Riesman too has turned to the necessities of policymaking in the 1960's through his concern over the problem of disarmament, a concern that operates for him in the larger context of what he calls the "American crisis." Here is something more than a simple extrapolation from the ideas of *The Lonely Crowd*. Instead of focusing on sociological determinants of personality types, Riesman sees the "American crisis" mainly in terms of a political phenomenon, the simplification of alternatives in American political life, the "dichotomizing tendency" in our political life.[3] The oversimplification of alternatives—the insistence on a choice between conformity

[3] David Riesman and Michael Maccoby, "The American Crisis," in *The Liberal Papers*, ed. James Roosevelt (Chicago: Quadrangle Books, Inc., 1962), pp. 34-36.

and individualism, slavery or freedom, democracy or communism, etc.—is what is working against "our need to plan distant as well as short-run goals." Thus we are unable to consider other possibilities and are trapped within simplistic definitions. But not only does Riesman concern himself with the problems of policy rather than of sociological character; he also believes that something might possibly be done about policy, or that at the very least it is necessary to try to change the American way of thinking about certain key issues. Thus he asks, How can the current ways of thinking about security in foreign and military affairs be changed? Rejecting downward manipulation of the public by the elite as simply another step in the destruction of an alert public and of creative alternatives, he turns to what he calls "lobbying 'upward.' " "Today, as free citizens, we need energetically to influence the military, industrial, political, and educational leaders into letting go of their investments in the cold war and into working not only for a safer but a better world."[4] Riesman's new concern for a liberalism that can operate in American society, and for a freedom composed in part of seeking for solutions to public problems, has downgraded the other-directed concept and upgraded the idea that there is or should be an American public composed of citizens.

Riesman's more recent interest in politics is still, however, deeply permeated by pessimism. Thus, writing in 1962 about the attitudes he expressed in 1950 in *The Lonely Crowd*, he says: "In emphasizing cultural and psychological matters, we implicitly made clear our lack of confidence in easy political remedies, although in urging individuals to 'feel free,' we understated the depth of our political despair. . . . Even if one recalls the relatively less oppressive and less terrifying political climate of 1948, it is hard to justify now the implicit as-

[4] *Ibid.,* p. 38.

sumption in *The Lonely Crowd* that the fragmentation of American political power by the veto groups and the political apathy of most Americans could be taken somewhat lightly. . . .[5]

Commenting on the problem today he says: "It would seem that men cannot live for long in a static, sober world drained of ideology—a world of veto groups and countervailing power and modest commonsensical gains within the system. . . . If in the 'developing' countries today men see ahead the goal of eliminating poverty and exploitation, in the 'overdeveloped' ones men become aware of more subtle frustrations, more indirect alienation. As yet, they see no way to make a political program out of personal demands for meaningful work, unphony personal relations, and unmilitaristic foreign policy."[6] In this situation "men no longer conspire enthusiastically in their own alienation: they are often somewhat disaffected, but they lack the conviction that things could be done any other way. . . ."[7] The sense of total dead end that these chilling sentences leave remains a key element in present liberal thought.

Thus he ends his consideration of the "American Crisis" by saying: "In order for us to live with our abundance, there must be greater participation in the political life of the United States and the world."[8]

C. Wright Mills in his last years also increasingly turned his attention to what were once called affairs of state. The problems of American foreign policy posed for him the need to awaken a public to the catastrophes into which they were being led by the power elite. In *The Causes of World War Three* (1960) and *Listen, Yankee* (1960) Mills poured out his

[5] Riesman, *The Lonely Crowd* (New Haven, Conn.: Yale University Press, 1961), pp. xxxiii, xxxv.
[6] *Ibid.*, p. xlvii.
[7] *Ibid.*, p. xxxix.
[8] *Ibid.*, p. 47.

scorn for those who dominate us. But he also attempted to grapple with the hard issues of Cuban policy and to understand the problems presented to America by change in the underdeveloped areas and by the arms programs of the two great powers. Along with Riesman and Goodman, Mills saw the need for concrete attitudes on public questions if the liberal belief in a free society was to be meaningful. Thus he tried to make the liberal see Cuba as presenting the political issue that emerges when a backward society tries to change and to construct a free society. "The real political issue of Cuba and in Cuba seems to me to be this: Is it possible by revolutionary means of the sort being used in Cuba to build a genuinely free society? Is it possible to carry through in such drastic and rapid ways a revolution as fundamental as this one without producing either revolutionary terror or permanent dictatorship?"[9] One may have grave doubts as to how Mills answered this question in regard to Cuba and still recognize that the attempt to face the question and to put it to the American public is based on the assumption that there is in fact a Yankee who will listen, that the power elite has not altogether won. One must also recognize, however, that Mills was still the most despairing of the social critics when he wrote these two works and that they were in a sense a last shot, a last attempt to avert what he saw as the ultimate victory of the power elite in America—and in Russia too.[10] By creating his own theoretical trap for himself in his sociological writings he could not find a way out. He is a tragic lesson in the ways by which social criticism can immobilize the liberal impulse.

The three leading social critics of America have turned

[9] C. Wright Mills, *Listen, Yankee* (New York: Ballantine Books, Inc., 1960), p. 184.

[10] For a significant and understanding consideration of Mills see Harvey Swados, "C. Wright Mills: A Personal Memoir," *Dissent*, Winter, 1963.

away from their concern with sociological theory and have focused on political issues of one sort or another. All of them have done so, however, in the frame of reference established by their theories. Goodman still has little faith in concrete political action. Hence his practical proposals avoid a discussion of the political system; all he can offer is a hope that perhaps people can be talked around by a candidate to adopt, for example, a plan for banning cars from Manhattan after they have been brought to see that it makes sense. Goodman does not understand that politics has a role in society; one can only assume that he would like to get rid of it as soon as possible. Riesman, on the other hand, now believes that veto groups can be moved to make important changes in policy. He has hopes that this is possible because he has discovered that American scholars and intellectuals incorrectly see congressmen and politicians in general as "cynical opportunists or . . . stupid windbags." One must wonder what kind of scholars and intellectuals he talks to; certainly such a statement only reveals his own political provincialism and does not give one much faith that his new interest in politics is very realistic. The most recent work of Mills, however, is even more unrealistic, since he rejected the whole political system as it stands in favor of fundamental and revolutionary change outside of the system. He had to reject the American political system because there was nothing left in it for free men according to his analysis.

Despite their deeply flawed views on politics, what is most important about the present involvements of these social critics is their concern with the affairs of society in terms of policy and political alternatives. Rather than removing themselves from history, society, and politics, they are making the effort to end their self-effacement and make liberalism into an ideology that has something to say to a public, to a citizen. Their necessary assumption that there is a public of citizens instead of mass men is in itself the most important sign of the change in liberal thought.

The Political Roles of the Liberal and Radical

In considering the possibilities of liberalism in the 1960's it is necessary to look for the moment at the different ways the liberal and radical act to bring about change. Up to now it has been feasible to discuss them in tandem because in the era of social criticism both arrived at fundamentally the same conclusions. But if liberalism is to become a doctrine of public affairs the unique methods by which the liberal and radical separately operate in public life must be revived.

The traditional function of the liberal in America has been that of the reformer, the man who spends his energies in changing the system in important particulars, but who generally gives little thought to changing it as a whole. He is opposed to the status quo but not necessarily opposed to the whole society of which he is a part. He is a man with a particular grievance or a particular interest. The grievance, it is worth noting, might be in someone else's interest rather than his own—one of his most endearing traits. Although a particularist, he is nevertheless capable of trenchant attacks and criticisms on some fundamental aspects of the system and, indeed, at times he can strike the radical pose most effectively; Bryan's Cross of Gold speech was for its time a not completely inaccurate piece of demagoguery, and Franklin Roosevelt's scorn about the crocodile tears of the economic royalists raised some interesting questions about capitalism—questions which, presumably, are no longer raised because we are all economic royalists now. Yet most reformers of the liberal persuasion in America have been a part of the system itself and have confined themselves to particularism except when the system maddened them by its blindness to its own self-interest; only then did they launch into demagogic excesses.

It is this particularism that is at once the weakness and glory of the liberal. The weakness is obvious enough today. By patching here and patching there and patching everywhere, liberals actually improve the fundamental social system and leave it in better shape than when they came upon it. But their effectiveness is limited not only to certain spheres of action but also to a certain period of time. When the particular need is fulfilled, the reformer and his movement lapses. The system absorbs him and his ideas, and he can even find himself in the queer position of becoming a defender of the past. The moving finger having writ moves on and leaves him sitting bemused among the scrolls of his success. Today, for example, Roosevelt's heirs are left with the legacy of prideful memories. More accurately, such an inheritance robs them of their legacy. A particular problem and a particular moment have passed; the reform movement died with their death.

Naturally it is assumed by the liberal that in this imperfect world there will always be *something* that needs reform, and, true enough, there usually is something. But particularism creates difficulties for itself; it is hard to know what it is that needs reform in an era of good-feeling when there is no immediate and overwhelming crisis. And even if a cause can be found, it may not be very important. The reformer is therefore distinctly susceptible, on the one hand, to a lack of continuity of effort, and on the other, to indulgence in empty sentimentality. The answer to such a problem is, of course, that if there is nothing to reform then the matter is settled. But, equally, such an answer fails when the social critics can show that the threat to freedom is greater than ever before *precisely because reform will not succeed.* In this situation the liberal is caught in the circle of his own reasoning, helpless, and filled with despair about himself and everyone else.

Yet there is virtue in his particularism. While it is true that the liberal may tend to fuss with the system rather than change it, it is also true that the total effect of his finicky reforms is considerable. That America in the 1960's is far different from America in the 1930's is the result of New Deal reforms. The change has been slow but it has been persistent, and has continued to work long after the New Deal died. The main bulwarks of our social and economic system, to be sure, have held constant throughout but the fact of significant change is testified to by the social critics themselves, who have had to develop a new approach to the study of society to deal with this "new" society. One may or may not like the direction of change initiated, and one may be discouraged by the fact that no one really seemed to be in charge of the direction of the change. But the effect of particularism in releasing change cannot be denied. Certainly it has been more potent in releasing change than the theories of the radicals.

The other virtue of particularism derives from the liberal's participation in the life of his times and his society. Reform requires involvement in the details of concrete problems; it requires specific knowledge of how institutions of all kinds operate and the ways in which they can be manipulated; it requires, finally, the creation of coalitions and leaders to achieve the object in view through political power. In these ways the liberal acts *in* society to bring about change and to increase the freedom of his fellow citizens. Through his particularism he participates in society and in history where both are created and come alive—in the realm of social decisions. He does more. He becomes someone who actually works with the men around him even though he may despair of them and their condition, or even of himself and his condition. For all his faults, the liberal as a reformer is *actively* concerned with those who live in his society.

In dealing with the minutiae of everyday life the liberal often loses his way and becomes a part of the system itself, allowing himself to be exploited. The radical, not concerned with detail, almost never loses his way. Rather he wanders off on his own and by himself. His role in American political life has been not to reform but to point out the radical defects of our society, the essence of our failures rather than the specifics of our problems. His sweep is wide, at times grandiose, his vision inclusive and holistic, his assumptions long-range and optimistic. Looking with a combination of scorn, amusement, and amazement at those who take reform seriously, he finds salvation—and salvation is often the word—only in a change of system rather than change in the system. He therefore stands apart in order to criticize and attack the system itself rather than its faults. While he is not necessarily a Jeremiah, he mainly sees history operating in terms of large-scale trends and developments that drastically change the face and essence of society from one epoch to another. The radical's role is therefore to wait for and aid drastic change.

The defect of the role springs from the task. To wait for and aid drastic change is not in itself impossible. What is nearly impossible is to stimulate a society or system to drastic change if the radical has lost faith in the people with whom he has to work within the society—its victims, in radical parlance—in order to overthrow it. Sectarianism of the most futile sort is often the result. The radical's vision splits him from those who are engaged in the system. But then, with whom is he going to work to overthrow it? Perhaps the forces of history will rescue him from his dilemma. But the forces of history are made up of human beings who act. And as the radical looks around, the only human beings he sees acting are those who are his enemies or at least not his allies. It is for this reason that radicalism has become an American synonym for ineffectiveness. The radical is more interested in the forward movement of history than the liberal or anyone else, and he is less capable of taking part in it than anyone else.

The virtue of the radical lies in his refusal to believe in the system and in his consequent inability to be taken in by it. Aware of the nature and failure of the system, he brings these to light in a way that the liberal is incapable of doing. Most important, his rejection, his ability to stand outside, creates an exhilaration that is necessary for any movement of politics and opinion to exist. The fact that radicalism refuses to be bound gives those who are its professors a significant measure of freedom even while they are of necessity living in the abhorrent system. Simply because they put themselves outside, they act out an experience of freedom that is denied the liberal. They thereby keep freedom alive in a situation that by their own analyses threatens its extinction. While the system is tottering to its ruin and carrying the liberal and his precious reforms with it, the radical maintains an area of freedom that is important precisely because it is not practical, precisely because it is of no use within the system. That the radical is able to spurn the system may well be in certain situations the only evidence that freedom still exists within it.

But, at the same time, he participates and acts within it in ways that may be different from those pursued by the liberal but that are nevertheless similar in their results. He is not often a reformer because he is far from the sources of power even in his own imagination. Rather his act of participation is achieved through his profound and acute sense of the nature and quality of society, which gives him a dimension of objectivity. Indeed, he is involved in society even more than the liberal because he has no vestige of that individualism that dogs even the most well-meaning twentieth-century American reformer. The radical is the social man par excellence; more than anyone else, he knows the worth of society and why it is necessary that the individual must sink himself in his society. Rather than trying to save the freedom of the individual as the liberal inclines to do, he tries to save the freedom of a whole society. The source of his radical thrust, of his undercutting the establishment and those liberals who must of necessity work with it, comes from his inability to believe that the society created by the establishment is a possible means of achieving freedom; it must therefore be replaced by a new society, not merely with men freed from the restraints of the old.

While social criticism is informed with much of this radical sense of the nature of freedom as a social phenomenon, and some of the qualities of liberal reform, it is a significant and unique phenomenon in the history of liberal and radical thought because it reduces the act of social participation to a minimum. By its portrayal of society as a fixed tyranny, it may keep alive a radical belief in freedom as a social product, but only in the most abstract and tenuous way. In its description of our time, society becomes so overwhelming, so dominant that it produces organization men, a power elite, and so forth, and that is all. Liberal reform thus becomes hopeless, for the social critic cannot contemplate the possibility of moving society forward by piecemeal change. Certainly it would be unjust to say that social criticism is opposed to the essence of liberalism and radicalism, if for no other reason than the fact that it yearns toward that essence. But it is not unjust to say that it is liberalism and radicalism at the end of their tether, with the quality of social participation almost refined out of existence.

A Twinge of Optimism

The task of the coming search for freedom is to reinvigorate and re-create on a new basis the political-social roles of the liberal (if, for convenience, we may now revert to our use of a common term for liberal and radical). The old basis of political existence is gone and social criticism is the historical record of its disappearance. Programmatic politics, the stirring up of national political movements are not feasible or likely today. Easy ideological solutions have withered in the face of complexities. Must one conclude, therefore, that the liberal role can no longer be played?

Since optimism is so decidedly out of fashion, it is hard to feel even a twinge of optimism in facing such a question. Nevertheless a twinge can be felt: the sharp pain of atrophied muscles suddenly stretched after a decade in a cramped position. Two facts reveal that the liberal is and can be relevant to public life.

First, there is the existence of concrete and significant problems in society today that are susceptible to concrete and significant solutions. They are all well-known; they range from urban renewal and mass education, to the presence of poverty and destitution among large groups of Americans. In addition, foreign relations pose such problems as what to do about Cuba, foreign aid, and the Western alliance. Threatened with imminent failure in these areas the liberal tends to get discouraged and hence apathetic about "what can be done." In addition he looks at them as second-order problems that are mainly of concern to the specialist. But he must deal with these failures of his society; he cannot afford to shrug them off. If he cannot at least make the attempt to resolve failure or to deal with second-order problems, it baffles the imagination how he is to exist in any effective way at all. For if he confines himself only to those first-order problems described by the social critics he will be locked in a stasis that will put paid to his role in society.

Once it was possible to put second-order problems in their place in a historical development and thereby conceive of them in terms of a first-order problem. Marxism seemed to accomplish such a feat. But that age is gone and done with. Today we must exist without the crutch of a great forward movement of historical forces that are known and labeled. Instead we must wander in the rag-and-bone shop of history, picking up whatever useful objects we can. The problems we live with now may be called second-order problems but they compose the history of our times, the only history we have. To scorn it as inferior history is to be unhistorical in the extreme. History is a series of second-order problems. Eventually a trend may emerge. But to those who make history, the fact of second-order problems is more evident than the existence of a trend. Liberal thought today as exemplified by the social critics has not yet been able to recover from the loss of a particular type of history, the grand historical trend. As a result it rejects the only kind of history available to it and thus compounds its loss. There is little reason to think that any other than second-order problems will emerge in the near future. Those who are waiting for the new Marx will have a long wait.

The role of these problems for the liberal today is to provide him with an opportunity for a participation in society, history, and politics that will move him toward resolving the dilemmas delineated by the social critics. Through the expansion of equality the restrictions on freedom that derive from the other-directed, the organization, the power elite, and all the rest will be lessened or removed. Freedom is a phe-

nomenon to be used for some purpose, such as seizing upon
the problems history has dumped on us and devising concrete
solutions that will give more significant choices to more
people. To deal with the problems of urban renewal, of
poverty, even of foreign aid, as a liberal, is to deal with them
in terms of equalitarianism. For if they are not dealt with in
such terms, others will deal with them in *their* terms, and the
result will be a further degeneration toward the conditions
described by the social critics, toward greater inequality and
narrowing of choice. Equalitarianism today has the sound of a
quaint slogan from a nineteenth-century past; it seems to be-
long to the period of the simplistic community. But equality
is not incompatible with an era of large-scale organization.
Rather, it can be developed throughout the various structures
of such a society and on all its levels. The only agency available
for this purpose—failing revolution—is the power of the central government. For the government, in contradistinction to
any other institution, has as its object service to the whole
nation in the interests of equalitarianism within the limits of
its constitution and those prescribed by a desire for efficiency.

The American public has been unwilling to face this qualitative distinction between the role of government and—to be
exact—big business. But for the liberal a recognition and employment of this unique trait of government is basic to his
approach to politics and it is a way of discovering his political
role in the era that is beginning to open. It is, if nothing else,
to do battle with the conservative on the ground where he is
most fatuous, his inability to understand what kind of a society he lives in. More important, it gives him an answer to the
question: "What is liberalism for?"

Because the social critics have manifested a sort of neo-
Jeffersonianism in their instinctive recoil from the big society,
the Great Society, they have failed to discover any political

role for the liberal. Especially when social theory has led them and their readers into a condition of the dead end it has been difficult to know where the liberal fits in. Yet the mystery is not so deep. Liberalism seeks to expand freedom for The Other, sometimes known as one's fellowman, as well as for oneself. To do this is to recognize the necessity of restraint in one area of social activity so that choice can be expanded in another; e.g., it may be necessary to restrain the growth of supermarkets in order that colleges and universities may grow instead. Positing a conflict between the claims of, say, education as against the distribution industry raises, however, the question of how these decisions are to be made. By fiat? But that is to destroy, clearly, the very freedom the liberal seeks. Hence he must maintain—and improve—a political system that is democratic so that decisions are as freely come to as is possible in a large-scale society.

We will see some evidence that our political system is capable of democratic decision-making over a period of time. It will not, however, be capable of such decisions if the liberal —who alone is capable of posing the issue—does not make the attempt to make decisions—to *act*—within the system. If there ever was a case of the self-confirming hypothesis, the liberal belief that the American political system is a failure is one. Somehow enough people have to be convinced—and the people involved will not necessarily be The People but may be a small group of legislators, etc.—that it is better to have shabby supermarkets than shabby universities. A difficult conviction to get across, to be sure.

It will be easier to get it across if the problem is seen not only or even mainly as a specific reform but in the context of government as a planning agency. Here is where the liberal with his sometimes single-minded fascination with particular problems can take some useful lessons from the radical. If he does so he will be able to put forward a concept of government as not only the key energizing agency in our economic affairs but the way in which society can operate today in the interests of the whole without a sacrifice of freedom, rather than operating as a supermarket. One excellent formulation of the question as it exists in British politics describes what is involved in planning by government:

Setting aside utopian goals of complete equality and total socialization, the current political line-up [in Great Britain] has to do with how much planning there should be, and who should be in charge of the machinery. Whatever may be said about the growth of managerialism, this is ultimately a political issue: in other words, a question of power. Very likely socialization need not everywhere take the form of nationalization—in the traditional sense. But it must take *some* [sic] form that is recognizably different from either private entrepreneurship or corporate management.[11]

The necessity of coming to grips with this question can even be put on the simple level of regaining ground lost in the 1950's, for the impact of the government in terms of achieving greater equality of income has diminished within the past decade. The distributional effect of taxes and benefits of both the national and state governments in the years 1950–1957 was to increase inequality. In addition, if national defense expenditures are omitted, both national and local governments used a smaller amount of the gross national product in 1956–1960 than in 1929–1933.[12] While the social critics had their backs turned on the American political sys-

[11] George Lichtheim, "Does Public Ownership Still Matter?" *Dissent*, Spring, 1963.

[12] According to Jacob Cohen and Morton Grodzins in "How Much Economic Sharing in American Federalism?" *American Political Science Review*, March, 1963. In 1929–1933, government expenditures, other than for national defense, were 12.72 per cent of the gross national product; in 1956–1960 they were 10.56 per cent.

tem some odd things have been happening to its impact on American society—things that should gladden the heart of the conservative. Clearly the role of government as a creator and molder of society is no more significant today than it was in the past—and it was not overwhelming then. Those conservatives today who complain about the all-powerful role of government are either ignorant—which is more likely than not—or pulling our leg. But whatever the case, the sad fact is that many liberals themselves have come to believe much of the conservative argument and have assumed that the role of government as an equalizing and distributive force was secure. But it is not secure. It is not secure because of antigovernmental conservatism and liberal passivity. In plain English: the conservatives have got what they want; the liberals have not.

Government—particularly national government—can be the institution through which a whole people express at one and the same time both their unity and their differences, can find embodiment of this particular and absolutely unique characteristic of democracy. In addition it can be an experience of a freedom that is not only different from the freedom to be experienced in a supermarket, but is, if one may be bold, qualitatively of a higher and more rewarding character. For it is an experience of choice that comes from the pursuit of worthwhile objects—making and changing a society, *our* society—and from working with one's fellowmen in the affairs of society through politics. The one builds a historic structure; the other is simply a decision between one trading stamp and another. The fact that the American public has been sold the idea that the supermarket is freedom is in itself enough to indicate the work that the liberal has to do.

The government is the only institution through which these values can be realized. It can of course be an engine of despotism and terror. But the liberal has become so frightened over the possible threats of government that he has failed to recognize it is the only way in which men can work together in both equality and freedom in a large-scale society. Democratic and constitutional governments are forced by their essence and by law to recognize all men as equal and—again —are the *only* institution to do so. They are also forced by their very essence and by law not merely to let men argue freely, not even merely to let them operate freely, but to bring them together as a common body of men who still retain their differences while they pursue a common objective. Hence it is the only institution by which men can act in society and in which they can make a history of their society through a search for freedom. Democratic and constitutional government is the only institution through which it is possible to engage in an adventure of invention for a whole people.

Thus the role of government for the liberal is not only to help the weak—important though that may be—but to act as a means by which the society as a whole undergoes the experience of being free. An endeavor by a democratic and constitutional government to carry out a project is an activity unlike that of any other institution because it must involve in one way or another—even if only through argument and disagreement—the whole society. Further, it creates whole new categories of activities that cannot be found in other institutions —valuable though those may be in their own particular spheres and necessary though they too may be to freedom.

What a vision and birthright the liberal—or anyone else, for that matter—gives up when he ignores the significance of government in a democratic and constitutional society! Vision? But what about reality? Indeed, reality is a far cry from the potential that government offers. But that reality will never move closer to the potential unless the potential itself is recognized. And only the liberal today, in the United States of the 1960's, has the ability to put forward and state at least some of the potential; only he has the ability to *teach* it.

There is a new image—vision is too hortatory a word—of government to be put before the American public. It is an image of government not as a referee, not as a despotism, not as an eleemosynary *cum* welfare institution. It is an image of government as a manifestation of a whole society that is engaged in pursuits important to society, freely chosen by a process of political interaction among those who compose society. It is an image that can be brought down to earth by facing the concrete issues of this particular moment of history and using them to engage both the public and the government in their solution. In the process the planning function of government will not only resolve certain specific problems but will teach the public that it is in fact a public, that as a public those who are a part of it have another role to play than that of sticking their snouts in the swill offered by the supermarkets, namely, to create a better society, a place where men can act freely with one another. The office of the liberal today is to drag at least some of the middle class in America, the group that is dominant in power and influence, away from its belief that government is something that scarcely bears thinking about, that at best it is a service organization for the unfortunate. The conversion of the middle class of America to a different view of what government means is a task for the liberal that can be achieved only through the seizure of particular issues and the clarification of his own ideology. That attitudes toward government can and have changed is manifest. Now there is an opportunity for another change. No one else will bring about that change if the liberal does not.

The second reason for believing that the liberal can have a political role today is the new postwar and post-Eisenhower generation, those who are now coming of political age. Although it is probably true that the population as a whole is not liberal in any significant political sense of the word, it is also at least possible that there is a "constituency" that can be moved by liberal ideas among the college students and the scientific intelligentsia of the colleges and graduate schools. Much has been said about the career orientation of this group. Little has been said about the effect of their training on their approach to the problems of society and to the question of achieving and protecting freedom in society. This group, with its keen sense of problem-solving and its highly developed sense of society, is of all the major groups in the population the one most likely to be involved in the coming search for freedom. It is essential to their existence as a scientific intelligentsia. It is they who will provide the purchase and the means and the image of freedom in an organized and complex system that will not only make problem-solving possible but also provide a drive toward equalitarianism. To ignore their vital role is to ignore one of the few trends of history working on the side of freedom.

The existence of a history made up of events and concrete problems, and of a potential constituency, will make it feasible for the liberal to realize his existence in terms of his unique desire and need to participate in the affairs of men. But to accomplish this act of participation, politics must be conceived not in terms of a simpleminded despair but of working within whatever situation lies at hand.

The Flexibility of Politics

Although much of what the social critics say about politics is germane, there is evidence from the world of politics itself, and from the political scientist and historian, that as a method of willed and rational change it is not totally blocked.

The possibilities of working within a situation have been shown by the Negro protest movement as it boiled over into action and demonstration in the spring and summer of 1963. What was perhaps most curious and interesting about this movement was the sudden speed with which our political leadership discovered that something must be done about the burdens under which the Negro has been laboring, a discovery made simultaneously on almost all levels of politics. It is tempting to come to the cynical conclusion that the response of American political leadership to Negro demands for legal rights is in direct ratio to the threat which the protest movement poses to the bourgeois sense of security and property, and that Northern political leadership panics at the sound of tramping feet. It is also worth pointing out that the efforts to crack the citadels of racism in the North, the middle-class and upper-class suburb, have hardly begun and that the President's civil-rights program of 1963 is limited and partial.

Yet such conclusions, morally cynical as they are, overlook three crucial aspects and lessons of the Negro protest movement of 1963. First, as against those who claim that politics in America is simply the playground of a power elite or of characterological types, it provided evidence that the elements for effective political action are lying around in our political system waiting to be fused together. These elements are many and include pressure groups, the courts, political parties, legislatures, public opinion, and the executive branches of our numerous governments. What the Negro movement has shown is how each and all of these can be fused or orchestrated to achieve a particular object over a period of time—a period which may be long or short and which has, therefore, a historical dimension. It has shown that these elements, though they seemed to have atrophied because they were not used together in pursuit of a common end, are in fact capable of life and energy. To say that it takes an explosion of

great force and power to fuse these elements and to release
their energy is simply to say what has always been true, that
politics is everywhere characterized by conservatism and stone-
walling unless it is forced to be otherwise. What is important
is that the act of fusion can take place in America, and that
we can now be released from the thrall in which social criticism has put us to explore other areas that might provide for
such a fusion.

Second, the agitation of 1963 has shown that a relationship
can be brought into being between the lower world of anarchy
and the upper world of bureaucratic insolence, that the exploited can communicate with the holders of power, and that
this communication—fragmentary though it may be—can
jump the gap between the marchers at the gate of the White
House and the occupant of the White House. Intentions, desires, and—most important of all—the intensity of those
desires can be made clear on the part of both sides. Out of
this communication a form of cooperation and working together—again fragmentary, informal, and incomplete—can
arise. This cooperation and quasi-organized working together
can give the one segment of political leadership which is
susceptible to a particular appeal the strength it needs to force
other segments to act. Let us give President Kennedy his due:
whatever his desires and intentions were in regard to civil
rights, it was virtually impossible for him to act effectively
until the Negro had cooperated (tacitly) by giving him a tool
with which to coerce those opposed to civil rights—namely,
the threat and fear of widespread civil disobedience.

Politics is a wondrous and complex thing, and cooperation
in political efforts is seldom neat and tidy. But it does come
into being under certain circumstances even between the
lowest and the highest in the land. The fact that it has done
so on the Negro question raises the possibility that the whole

realm of political action may be opening up to the liberal once again. The Negro movement may lead to the creation of a wider liberal political movement that will postulate an increased role for government in other areas of American life as a means of achieving specific goals; it may lead to an ideological vision—if one may mention that discredited word—of an America that is something other than a paradise for General Motors.[13] If this is to happen it will be necessary for the Negro to see his own problem in the light of a potential development of a liberal political movement. For his own particular problem is part of a larger problem in America, the problem of exploitation by a system which cares only to sell its goods. Especially in the North, segregation is simply one element in a complex comprised of slums, inferior education, miserable cities, and lack of planning. Millions of dollars for super-highways and office buildings, not to mention expensive apartments, but very little for Negro education is a problem not of segregation as such but of the political power of the groups which dominate our urban areas.

Finally, the civil-rights movement has demonstrated that government, and more particularly the national government,[14] is the vital ingredient in achieving significant change in America. Voluntarism and mass agitation are essential but they are effective only if they eventuate in governmental action and are linked with it through law and law enforcement. The sequence of the civil-rights movement has been one of its most significant features. Starting with action by the judicial

[13] Walter Lippmann, always a bellwether of intellectual fashion, has said: ". . . it will prove to be impossible to approach the equality of opportunity for Negroes without reviving and renewing the progressive movement which has been quiescent for some ten years, . . ." *Newsweek*, July 8, 1963.

[14] See John P. Roche, "The Curbing of the Militant Majority," *The Reporter*, July 18, 1963, and Henry Steele Commager, " 'To Form a Much Less Perfect Union,' " *The New York Times Magazine*, July 14, 1963, on the role of centralized government in America as a protector and creator of liberty.

branch of the government in conjunction with prior organizational and pressure-group activity by the NAACP, it moved
into the streets and to a climax of mass protest. It then became
a political affair in which the President and Congress were
intimately involved.

Certainly voluntary action still has a crucial role if only
because it is a means of goading the government into the use
of its power. But it must be directed toward the manipulation
of that power. Thus, the suburbs will open up to the Negro
only when the government forces the real estate dealers to
offer houses to everyone. Law, the enforcement of law, and
the power of government to organize society are the prerequi-
sites which the liberal must learn to use for his ends rather
than allowing the conservative to use them. The liberal must
learn not to burke the fact that coercion through legal processes will be necessary if not only Negro rights but other
objectives are to be achieved.

The idea that the power of government is a means to social
objectives is in direct conflict with the bourgeois dream of
minimum government and quasi-anarchy. It offers the liberal
the objective of another kind of America, one in which society
acts in such a way that it can be proud of its achievements as
a society rather than as the achievement of a private company.
The Negro protest movement has shown, once again, how the
government can be used to posit and achieve objectives for a
whole society because it is the only organization concerned
with the whole society.

What has happened, in fact, as a result of this movement
substantiates the findings of some political scientists and historians who, unlike the social critics, see opportunities for
significant change occurring through politics. They are able
to discover those opportunities because they reject the simple
definition of democracy as Rule by The People. Hence it is

also possible for them to reject the despair that accompanies the discovery that politics is a complex, cumbersome, and tortuous process that seemingly destroys or obscures what The People want. Instead, politics can be seen to possess dynamic qualities in which a play of conflicting factors, tendencies, and groups brings about change. In this process basic shifts of public opinion take place over long periods of time that create entirely new and different ways of thinking about society. These shifts involve the presence of "influentials," directors and informers of public opinion found on all levels, wherever leadership is necessary and possible. Their presence shatters the concept of a power elite and provides society, in V. O. Key's terms, with "democratic activists" who "consist of people arranged along a spectrum of political participation and involvement, ranging from those in the highest posts in official leadership to the amateurs who become sufficiently interested to try to round up a few votes for their favorite in a political campaign."[15] Rather than being passive, inert, and exploitable, from this point of view society becomes an organized system possessing the ability to make up its mind and change its mind.

Such is the picture of public opinion that emerges from V. O. Key's *Public Opinion and American Democracy*. Looking at the problems of politics in America, he comes to a qualified belief in the ability of a democracy to direct its own affairs through a process of political interaction among political leaders of all varieties, low as well as high in the social scale. It is from this interaction that change in American political attitudes and activities has come about. It is also this process of interaction that opens politics to some degree at least to whomsoever wishes to lead. The results of a particular act of

[15] V. O. Key, Jr., *Public Opinion and American Democracy* (New York: Alfred A. Knopf, Inc., 1961), p. 552.

leadership may not be much at a particular moment of time
but there is reason to hope that cumulative efforts can have a
cumulative and circular impact.[16] Thus Key can say:

> ... Our analysis of the American scene cautions us against easy
> acceptance of [a] glib theory of the dynamics of democratic self-
> destruction. We have pictured public opinion as the product of
> an interaction between political influentials and the mass of the
> people, an interaction that may produce alterations in mass opin-
> ion. In the course of time that interaction may also alter the
> modal position of the influentials as a novel doctrine asserted by
> one sector of the influentials gains acceptance among the masses.
> Mass opinion is not self-generating; in the main it is a response
> to the cues, the proposals, and the visions propagated by the
> political activists.[17]

In this analysis the elite is replaced by the "influentials." Because the latter lack homogeneity they permit a healthy tension and conflict to develop in American public life. Key can
see the possibilities for freedom and variety in America: "A
wide range of discretion exists for whatever wisdom leadership echelons can muster in the public service."[18] The gap
between his concept of change and that of the social critic is
clearly revealed by his statements that "mass opinions, aspirations, and expectations change as the political system moves
through time," and that "it is in this moving situation that
the power of mass opinion makes itself manifest in its inter-
actions with democratic leadership."[19] Thus his picture of
American public opinion is not one of a monolithic mass directed from above but of blocs of opinions changing through
time and interacting with one another and with a variety of

---

[16] For a description of a theory of circular and cumulative causation—a
theory significantly different from any put forward by the social critics—
see Gunnar Myrdal, *Economic Theory and Under-Developed Regions* (London: Gerald Duckworth and Co., Ltd., 1957).

[17] Key, *op. cit.*, p. 557.

[18] *Ibid.*, p. 555.

[19] *Ibid.*, p. 554.

influentials. It is a picture of complexity, of variety, and of
flexibility. It is also a picture in which a sense of community
can be discovered, a sense that a "greater common interest
should prevail."[20] The public is not so easily duped by its own
private concerns as it might seem; there is actually a sense of
"the collectivity." Inchoate it may be; naïve and inadequate
it may appear to the sharp sophisticated eye of the social critic;
but the fact of its existence as proven by Key's analysis should
be celebrated as providing something with which to work.

The rejection of naïveté can lead to sober and more hopeful conclusions than the old bromide, "In a democracy the
people should rule; the people do not rule; therefore there is
no democracy." E. E. Schattschneider does not think the
people do or can rule; he thinks they are simply "semisovereign." In his *The Semisovereign People,* he tells us without
equivocation that he is presenting "an attack on all political
theories, all research techniques and concepts tending to show
that American politics is a meaningless stalemate about which
no one can do anything."[21] An exhilarating statement. And
he therefore points to the immense changes which have in
fact taken place in the American system of government "while
we were thinking about something else." In his view the
changes in our system "could hardly have been greater if we
had had a violent revolution."[22] The American governmental
system, he tartly observes, "seems to be highly flexible." The
source of that flexibility he identifies as conflict within the
political system, which, even when it takes the form of "un-
resolvable" conflicts does not, however, produce a stalemate;
"the equilibrium is dynamic"[23] because conflict is not only

[20] *Ibid.,* p. 549.
[21] E. E. Schattschneider, *The Semisovereign People: A Realist's View of
Democracy in America* (New York: Holt, Rinehart & Winston, Inc., 1961),
p. viii.
[22] *Ibid.*
[23] *Ibid.,* p. 125.

significant within the government but is more significant between the government as a whole and other power systems
(i.e., business). Thus alternatives in the American system are
kept alive. "Democracy as we know it today depends on the
way in which the political and economic powers are played off
against each other, the way we steer a course between domination and subservience. We need not be dismayed to find that
business is powerful. Power is inherent in modern business
organization. The object of the game is not to destroy business
power but to match it with governmental power."[24]

Schattschneider, quite correctly, would seek not to destroy
organization in a fit of neo-anarchistic fury but to use it in
terms of democratic goals, to take advantage of modern
organizational structure for democracy rather than retreat
into personal autonomy. And the way it can be done is
through the power of government. That, in the domestic
arena, is what politics is about, for the role of democracy has
been to "provide the public with a second power system, an
alternative power system, which can be used to counterbal-
ance the economic power."[25] The people are semisovereign
not because they are ignorant; in Schattschneider's view only
the intellectuals who condemn the people are ignorant—an
interesting and unsettling thought. It would be stupefying if
it turned out that it is not the people who are naïve but the
intellectuals and the social critics. The people, rather, are
semisovereign because they do not know everything about the
problems facing governments but know a good deal because
they are involved in the conflict systems of politics. Schattschneider puts the point in simple terms so the least profound
intellect can grasp it: "The people are involved in public
affairs by the conflict system. Conflicts open up questions for

[24] *Ibid.*, p. 127.
[25] *Ibid.*, p. 121.

public intervention. Out of conflict the alternatives of public policy arise."[26] Thus, the problem that faces democracy in the struggle for power no longer seems the insuperable one posed by the social critics. It is a problem of organizing the political system so that the public can operate to choose alternatives, a task that in turn requires "a tremendous effort to define the alternatives, to organize the discussion and mobilize opinion."[27] Such is the role of government and the political parties.

Certainly, the achievement of that task is not simple, but it at least is concrete; it is subject to the energies of man, and does not pose the hopeless rigidities that the social critics would force on us and that instead of holding out possibilities simply crushes them.

The possibility of possibilities is increasingly beginning to attract intellectual opinion, and today there are others who reject the sterilities of the social critics in an effort to look around the landscape and see what can be done, what other ways there are of seeing our society. Indeed, there is an entire body of opinion that is working against the hopelessness of rigidity. A sense of the possibility and fruitfulness of conflict, in some cases pragmatic, in others, ideological, is creeping across the land.

The change in mood is noticeable in a notably even-tempered work by Edmond Cahn who approaches the subject of democracy from a legal point of view; he finds that men are responsible in a democracy and, more important, can assume their responsibility. *The Predicament of Democratic Man* does not tell us that the predicament is unbearable or leave us straddling a dilemma that cannot be resolved. Instead Cahn tries to find some reason to believe that the legal system can

[26] *Ibid.*, p. 138.
[27] *Ibid.*, p. 139.

produce a moral life in a democracy. To be moral assumes the possibility of guilt and Cahn makes it clear that the citizen assumes guilt for what his government (and one may add, his society) does. The guilt is not, however, and most emphatically, unlimited; government officials can also be guilty and hence can be evaluated by the citizen. Therein lies the hope of changing the citizen from a floating cipher to an active judge and participant in government. To make the citizen the carrier of all the wrongs of his government is to make his situation so hopeless that the only rational reaction on his part is to withdraw from the whole project into his private garden.

Thus Cahn restores, if one may say so, the people to government. Democratic government no longer seems impossible; the people are semisovereign because the responsibility is not theirs alone. Cahn sees that the officials of government have their responsibility too, in this case that of carrying out the law. But this does not mean that they alone govern; there is an interaction between the government and the people. The people do not govern; they sit in judgment on those who govern and they choose their governors by their moral judgment. It is possible that this can be done. Such is the assertion of Cahn. And in making that assertion and in giving evidence for it he tells us that democracy is possible, that beyond the world of veto politics, power elites, absurdity, and organization men there is a citizen making limited judgments that he can make stick.

. . . Democratic man's complete freedom of thought and his almost complete freedom of discussion serve to liberate not only his inner life but also his social transactions. . . . How does [he] proceed to develop the social regulations that he is expected to obey? By summoning the very mechanisms of thought, conscience, and communication . . . and using them to establish a continual flow of opinion between citizen and citizen and reciprocally between citizenry and officialdom, culminating at intervals in the formal mandates of the ballot box.[28]

Cahn even goes so far as to say that when the citizens are associated together, no matter how callous and ignorant they may be separately, they become as the people "the only dependable judges. . . ."[29] It is a stunning statement of the practical virtues of politics as a social act.

Evidence of an increased concern with flexibility comes from other areas of study besides the purely political. A historian tells us that history is a way of breaking the chains of the past, a way of moving beyond consensus. John Higham's "Beyond Consensus: The Historian as Moral Critic,"[30] puts aside the relatively recent conservative trend of interpreting American history and posits not a return to the naïveté of the pragmatism of the Progressives but instead an interest in both consensus and conflict out of which the historian becomes a moral critic. History becomes now the study of conflict rather than an assertion that men in the past incorrectly thought there was conflict, as such consensus-seekers as Daniel Boorstin, Clinton Rossiter, Louis Hartz, and Robert E. Brown have claimed. "In confronting all that is unstable and precarious in human values, [the historian] can discover the profoundest struggles and conflicts that the drama of history affords."[31] In his criticism of those who see America-as-consensus Higham displays an awareness of variety and complexity as the proper province of historical study, and the consequent need for the historian to possess a "complex awareness [to] take the place of systematic theory."[32]

Another approach on similar lines, which does not, how-

[28] Edmond Cahn, *The Predicament of Democratic Man* (New York: The Macmillan Company, 1961), p. 186.

[29] *Ibid.*, p. 167.

[30] John Higham, "Beyond Consensus: The Historian as Moral Critic," *The American Historical Review*, April, 1962.

[31] *Ibid.*, p. 625.

[32] *Ibid.*

ever, eschew systematic theory, is presented by a sociologist who stresses the role of variety and complexity as the necessity and fact of American pluralism. William Kornhauser's *The Politics of Mass Society* describes a mass society as one in which a multiplicity of groups and other plural attachments ("intermediate relations") has disappeared so that elites and non-elites are accessible and available, one to the other. Contrariwise, in a liberal-pluralist society (i.e., the democratic society of the West) the non-elites are protected from manipulation by the elites through their intermediate groups. As a theory, Kornhauser's contribution ranks as a major conceptual discovery, but what is of interest here is his postulate that complexity and variety, i.e., pluralism, is of the essence in avoiding a mass society and his belief that in America such variety and complexity of intermediate groups is secure enough to establish the grounds for democracy. While the evidence for the latter belief is less impressive than the theory of mass society itself, it is nevertheless a counterstatement to the belief that we live in a rigidly structured society that lacks the potentialities that variety can bring.   •

Perhaps the best summary of what this flexibility can mean for freedom is found in the remarks of an Englishman, Richard Hoggart, in his discussion of the role of the intellectual in a society seemingly bent on massification. Pointing out that an intellectual must not act just as a "general moral mentor," Hoggart seeks a role for him that can put to use whatever flexibility may exist in society as a whole. The intellectual, he tells us, must "sustain a critical and creative probing of the life of his time," in order "to work more within society, actively and pragmatically . . . so as to create institutional safeguards against the worst . . . effects of a mass consumers society. There is no shortage of good issues—in education, in the social services, in the organisation and control of the mass media and elsewhere. . . ."[33] Hoggart goes on to say that the role of the intellectual, therefore, is to "help devise, within the organisation of society, areas which will encourage decent development," and that he should "realize that a potential audience for . . . 'reasonable and truthful' speech does exist."

Such action as he suggests could mainly come about through the use of the flexibility of a political system. Instead of creating social theories about our misery the intellectual could use the political system to attack those who hold power to no significant ends. He could also use the system to try to speak to those who are exploited by it. What if it were only a verbal dialogue and attack? It would be better than no dialogue and attack and it is sometimes surprising how a verbal attack can stymie the members of a governing elite, an elite that, on the whole, is not very bright. And verbal attacks may even broaden out into a more directly political attack since politics is never totally predictable. Also it must be remembered that there are those among the governing elite who are as nauseated by what society threatens to become as the social critic himself.[34] To "work more within society, actively and pragmatically," is at one and the same time to grasp the instrument that lies at hand—the political possibilities of democratic government—and to transcend a stultifying insistence on totalistic theory. Perhaps British empiricism rather than Weberian ideal types will save us yet.

Perhaps. One must not, however, ignore the terrifying incapacity of American politics. V. O. Key, Jr., for example, has no illusions.

[33] Richard Hoggart, "The Nostalgic, the Narkers, and the Knowing," *Encounter*, April, 1962, p. 62.
[34] One must be careful in this respect to discriminate between those who are really nauseated by the system and those who are simply worried by the threat the system poses to their own position as members of the elite.

In the short run . . . a multiplicity of cleavage may promote stasis if not paralysis within the state. By multiplication of the uncertainties and the risks for leadership, by subjection of elites to conflicting pressures and directives of dubious clarity, by creation of blocs of opinion susceptible to diversionary exploitation, a set of circumstances conducive to blockage of action comes into being. . . . Without determined and venturesome leadership, the great leviathan may stall on dead center. All this is not to deny that the Republic may, under some circumstances, flourish even though the government is stalled on dead center. The analysis points, rather, to the nature of the checks and balances within the social structure that have to be neutralized when major action becomes necessary.[35]

Riesman himself could not have put the point better—with one important exception. Key assumes at least the possibility of governmental leadership neutralizing the checks and balances of the social structure; Riesman assumes that the government will be and is simply the reflection of those checks and balances. It is difficult, however, not to feel that the American political system, especially since the end of World War II, has often been disappointing in the realm of domestic affairs (as contrasted with foreign affairs) and so less favorable to the liberal than to the conservative.

Yet it remains true that there is every reason to believe that politics in the United States today possesses more flexibility, more resources for change, than meets the eye of the social critics and those who despair of freedom. It is an opening, a means of experimentation and innovation, that, certainly, is difficult of access and slow of achievement, but that has the quality of moving history on a bit. Through the manipulation of political institutions on both the national and local level— both governmental and party—the liberal can make his voice heard and sometimes his influence felt. Through the creation

[35] Key, *op. cit.*, p. 178.

of issues he can not only affect a particular problem but contribute to the process of establishing a new ethos concerning the nature of government and society.

To these ends the liberal has a unique contribution to make.

The Resurgence of the Liberal

In the light of the flexibility possible to politics, the liberal can find some basis for believing that his role, his particular way of approaching society, is not after all hopeless. It may be feasible once again to look around and see not only what needs to be done, since that is obvious enough, but to recognize that it can be done.

The liberal idea of reform—piecemeal, cautious, and often naïve—can come into its own, ironically, in an age when the grand sweep of change is seen to be at a minimum. In such periods of history the liberal is most useful, but his potential depends on specific activities within the political arena. That arena is open to him today as always since it offers the chance of limited change. In such areas as urban renewal, foreign aid, education, and communications, he can exercise his penchant for limited improvement. In doing so he will not remake the world; he will not seem to touch on the issues raised by other-direction, the power elite, and all that. But he will change the society in which we live, and in doing so will keep liberalism and freedom alive by restoring them to the realm of history and society.

He must recognize that he can no longer be the monolithic leader of the nineteenth century who fancied himself engaged in sweeping reforms. But the erosion of other-direction and all the rest is not and should not be the crucial issue for the liberal. It is necessary for him to cease viewing our society as characterized by a single, all-encompassing syndrome. Instead, by acting out his role as a reformer he will *by that very act* at least cease to be other-directed, to be a victim of the power elite, to be absurd. Maybe the citadels of other-direction will remain, but at least he as a liberal will be involved with history and society. It is necessary to think of engagement not in the tradition of French *engagement* and revolution, but in the sense of liberal acts within a concrete situation.

Yet there are aspects of our situation—overdrawn though they may be by the social critics—that reform does not touch. Here the role of the radical becomes one of continuing to point out the insufficiency of reform and to organize his own politics dedicated to the principle that whatever is done isn't enough. The radical can perform some political acts that the liberal is incapable of performing by organizing political protest, which, as we have seen, can be uncommonly effective in our quasi-organized society. The act of protest in itself is useful in the situation we have because it refers to a politics of opposition of some kind no matter how "unsuccessful" that politics may be. In creating a radical opposition the theories of the radicals can become more than academic exercises performed for an academic audience.

The possibilities of liberal reform and radical protest are evident today because in fact both are operating—under a rather low head of steam, to be sure—with renewed force after the fatuous fifties. The reforming urge runs deep in American life, and in fact has never completely disappeared. The same is true of the radical protest movement. They both came to a standstill when they were replaced by social criticism, and their revival today is a process that may be just beginning. But that revival will be more potent and better sustained if there is some intellectual appreciation of how freedom is lost when society, history, and politics are lost.

The Experience of Freedom

Opportunities exist in America for the experience of freedom through its actual use. There is little possibility today for a grand liberal movement dedicated to principal and power; all that is likely are groups in one place or another working on a variety of concrete issues. And they will only be known as liberals by their willingness to innovate and experiment, to reject a return to a comfortable past, and by their desire and efforts to make it possible for more men to live in equality and freedom rather than in numbness and exploitation. It will hardly be an invincible army. But, despite all that the social critics have said and, in the face of their most despairing and anguished lucubrations, the upper world of bureaucratic insolence will find it impossible to suppress them. Most Americans, one may guess, are hardly liberals today. But there are enough to allow for minority movements to do their work. Dissent has not yet been crushed in America beneath the dull and stupid weight of the upper world.

For dissent to be significant the lower world of anarchic freedom must learn to use it in terms of a public life. The issues with which it will have to work may not be those that the liberal would like. But by using them as a means of expressing himself in public life he will be able to create an experience of freedom different from that put forward by the social critics. It will be an experience of freedom in terms of contact and conflict between the liberal on the one hand and the upper world of bureaucratic insolence on the other. It will be a search for ways to achieve greater equality of power and choice in a bureaucratic society. The social critics themselves have shown the need for this experience of freedom, but they also established a pessimism so total that action in public affairs became an absurdity.

The era of the social critics is now at an end. It is now possible to recognize the role of the liberal as an agent of society, as a maker of history. Liberalism by its very nature can have no eternal principles. But historically it has been a movement that sought to attain the largest area of freedom, of choice, for as many as possible. To do that meant a struggle for a society within which men could experience choice. The task that will be faced in the coming era of liberalism will be how to make this aim concretely relevant and feasible in a time of large-scale and bureaucratic organization. The liberal will have to achieve that goal while he carries a heavy burden of distrust of The Other and even of himself. It is a burden worth carrying because the destruction of illusion is always a necessary preliminary to working within a real world. But the destruction of illusion cannot be allowed to become a way of avoiding the real world of public life. The possibilities before the liberal today offer the chance of a new era—an era in which he will come to grips with the reality of history and society through the politics of working with his fellowmen.

Index